Oddities & Rarities
Michigan Back Roads

Have Fun

by

Ron

Ron Rademacher

Revised Edition

Back Roads Publication
P.O. Box 458
Rapid River, Michigan 49878

PAGE NUMBERS MAP

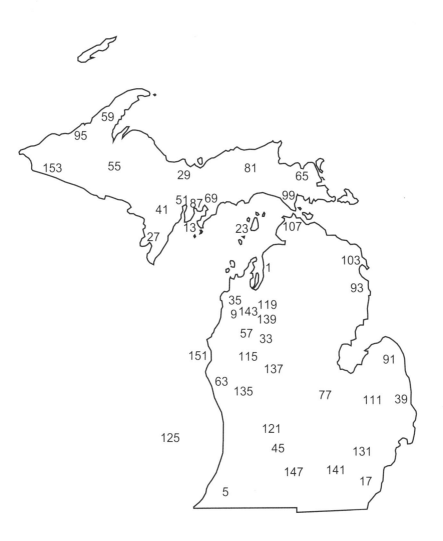

TABLE OF CONTENTS

Oddities & Rarities
Michigan Back Roads

by

Ron Rademacher

Back Roads Publications
P. O. Box 458
Rapid River, Michigan 49878

Acknowledgments

No book is the work of just one person. This one wouldn't have been written without the unwavering support and suggestions of the sponsors.

Cover Photograph – Newberry Statue
Ron Rademacher

Thanks are due to all the folks in the small Michigan towns who have made time for my presentations, endless questions, and photographic intrusions.

A special thanks to the people and organizations who supported and sponsored this project.

Proofreading by Kathy Jacobs

Oddities & Rarities
Michigan Back Roads

by Ron Rademacher

Published by
Back Roads Publications
P. O. Box 458
Rapid River, Michigan 49878

ISBN-13: 978-0-9883138-6-6

A PALACE – A FICKLE HEART

In the 1880s Robert Richardi, a German immigrant, built a factory in Bellaire, Michigan to produce wooden ware, some based on his own patents. The factory was extremely modern for the times, drawing power produced from a dam on the nearby river. They made high quality wooden kitchen utensils for the most part. At one time the factory employed more than 140 people. In 1890 the factory burned down and Robert decided to leave the area. He left the company to his son Henri.

Henri continued to work in the area and wanted to get started on a family. He had met, and fallen in love with a beautiful woman, during a trip to Germany. He proposed marriage, but she was hesitant to move to the northern Michigan wilderness from her home in a metropolitan German city. Henri persisted, and promised to build her the most beautiful house in the state, if she would marry him. The lady told him to build the house first. Then she would come to America and marry him. He got right to work.

Henri Richardi proceeded to build a Victorian style house, the likes of which had never been seen, in the wild lumber country. Nothing was considered too good for his bride-to-be. The rooms were paneled with fine hardwoods, there was indoor plumbing, a central heating and cooling system, and electric lights. These were refinements that were unheard of at the time. The claim could be made that this was the country's first electric home, and it was run from the hydroelectric dam at the river.

Fireplaces with carved mantels, hardwood pocket doors, and beautiful wall paper, all combined to produce a spectacular interior. The exterior is just as stunning with towering cupolas and intricate gingerbread wood work. After years of work, the labor of love was complete. Henri sent photos of the incredible home to his love. Alas, she declined to be impressed and refused to leave home and marry him. With a broken heart, Henri boarded up the house and never even lived in it.

The house is still there today, and is considered one of the top examples of Queen Anne architecture in the entire country. What is more, is that, you can not only tour the house, you can stay there. It is now a Bed and Breakfast, the Grand Victorian. Many of the original details have been preserved including much of the hand crafted woodwork, the likes of which we probably won't see produced again.

The Bellaire Historical Museum is downtown, and houses a rich collection of photos and artifacts from the period during which the house was built. Included is an exhibit of those famous wooden implements from the old Richardi factory.

Directions: The Grand Victorian is on the edge of downtown Bellaire, Michigan. Trust me, you can't miss it. Bellaire is in Antrim County in the northwest of Michigan just east of Torch Lake on Route 88.

BEAR

CAVE

IS

THE

ONLY

CAVERN

IN

THE

LOWER

PENINSULA

BEAR CAVE

Bear Cave is located on the St. Joseph River, just a few miles north of Buchanon in Southwest Michigan. The cave was formed over 10,000 years ago, as a result of the glacial drift, and is the only cavern in Michigan. The receding glacier left behind Tufa and boulders which make up the construction of the cave. This is not a gigantic cavern, such as those found at Mammoth Cave, or the Carlsbad Caverns. Rather this is a small natural cave with multiple rooms. The whole thing is only about 150 feet.

Touring the cave doesn't take very long, but there are many details and unusual formations throughout the caverns. There are fossils embedded in the ceiling and walls, glacial boulders, and Cave Pearls. There is also a reddish gel-like substance that is iron oxide. It was used by the local Potawatomi Indians as a pigment for dyes.

As you descend the winding stairs into the cavern, you will see a Kansas Boulder thought to be tens of thousands of years old. The passage is about six to eight feet wide, damp, and more than ten feet high. The Tufa deposits that make up the cave walls are about 18 feet thick. While damp, the way is well lit, and the various formations are well marked, to add to the experience.

Toward the back of the cave is a secondary passage that leads to a room with a low ceiling and a large pool of crystal clear water. Beyond the low ceiling and pool is another hidden room. This room is known as the "Slave Room", because it was used to hide slaves making their way to freedom on the "underground railroad". This room also is home to the largest population of Eastern Pipistrelle Bats in lower Michigan. It doesn't happen often, but you might see a bat during your walk through the cave.

Local lore has it that the cave was used by bank robbers. The story is told that bandits robbed a bank in Ohio back in 1895. They made their way across the state line and hid out in the cave. That incident led to the cave being used to film the movie "Great Train Robbery" in 1903.

Bear Cave is located within the grounds of the Bear Cave RV Resort. So there is ample parking, security, and more to see during your visit to the cave. Follow the wooden boardwalk around the outside walls of the cave and you can walk by one of only 3 waterfalls in the entire lower peninsula. It may only be a few feet high, but this small plunge falls pours it on and after a good rain it will cascade right onto the boardwalk. Continuing on that walkway will bring you to a great scenic view of the St. Joseph River.

A visit to the cave wouldn't be complete without taking a short walk across the ravine to visit the "Tulip Tree". The tulip tree is enormous and sits on a high bluff above the river. The size of this tree alone makes it worth a visit, but like everything else around the area, there is some interesting history associated with this tree. Local legend says that this particular tree was an important meeting spot for councils of the Potawatomi Indians. The location of the tree would make it an ideal spot for watching traffic, friendly and otherwise, on the river. This would also make the spot a good location for tribal conferences since it would be easy to find for travelers.

The huge limbs of the tulip tree seem to be bent in unusual ways. Some say that the branches were bent by generations of braves sitting, or standing on them, while keeping watch over the approaches to the sacred gathering spot. Another possible explanation for the bent branches, is that they were bent and twisted deliberately by the tribe. There are trees with deliberately bent branches near Horton Bay that form a circle that was used as a sacred council place. On Beaver Island are trees that have similarly bent branches that were bent that way, as directional markers, by nomadic tribes traveling the archipelago.

Directions: The Cave is located a couple miles north of Buchanan on the Red Bud Trail.

BOTTLE HOUSE

One of the most unique buildings in Michigan, was the result of a happy accident. The bottle house in Kaleva, Michigan, isn't a place to buy bottles or alcohol. It is one of the last remaining structures, in Michigan, that used bottles, as a primary construction component. John Makinen, operated a bottling plant, in Kaleva. The "happy accident" was, that he noticed that soda pop in bottles, stored in his warehouse, didn't freeze during the cold, northern Michigan winters. It was by this observation, that he discovered the insulating properties of his bottles, and that gave him an idea. He thought there just might be a use, for the thousands of flawed and chipped bottles, that were set aside, during quality control inspections.

Mr. Makinen was an inventive man. He created a special cementing mixture, that could be used, to bind the bottles together into walls. With that process, he set about using more than 60,000 of his bottles, to build his home, which became known as the Bottle House. Being artistic, as well as industrious, John Makinen wove different colored bottles, into designs and words, in the walls of the house, including the words, "Happy Home", on either side of the front door. The bottle house was popular, and neighbors had him build a few other structures around town, but they have all been torn down. The Bottle House is still there, and is now the Historical Museum. While touring the inside, the bottles are not visible, since the walls are finished, like any other home of the period. The insulating property of the bottles, comes in handy on a hot summer day. The 10 inch thick walls, keep the indoor temperature a good 10 degrees cooler, than outdoors.

William Makinen, John's brother, was also a manufacturing artist. He created the Makinen Tackle Company, to produce fishing lures. In 1945, Makinen Tackle, sold 135,000 lures. By 1946, the company had expanded to fifty employees. The Makinen Tackle Room, inside the Bottle House Museum, is dedicated to the company he created.

Another exhibit, inside the museum, kind of hidden away in a small room, is a genuine treasure. On the walls, are six colorful murals, created by school children, as part of the Work Projects Administration program. In addition, to being beautiful, these murals are unique, in that, they depict the Kalevela. The Kalevela, is the Finnish creation story. Written records of the Kalevela, in English, are difficult to find. These gorgeous murals, show the creation of the world, populated by dwarfs, princesses, gods, goblins, and a host of other mythical creatures. The murals alone are worth the trip to Kaleva, but there is more to see. There are other historic structures, and there are large, outdoor sculptures, scattered around town, including a giant grasshopper. It all makes for a great day trip.

THERE

ARE

ONLY

TWO

MICHIGAN

BOTTLE

STRUCTURES

STILL

STANDING

BURNT BLUFF PICTOGRAPHS

The Garden Peninsula, on Big Bay de Noc, is famous, as the location of a Michigan ghost town, Fayette. Fayette was an iron producing community and has been lovingly preserved. It is now an historic State Park, visited by thousands every year. There is another great treasure on this peninsula. Nearly forgotten, are the prehistoric cliff paintings, up on Burnt Bluff. The cliff paintings, pictographs at a sacred site, are located up on the cliff side, at and around, Spider Man Cave. Like Fayette, this site was a popular tourist attraction. Unlike Fayette, this site had no protections at all.

Burnt Bluff is a limestone cliff, on the shore of Big Bay de Noc, similar to those visible at Fayette. The bluff is about 150 high. Spider Cave is about 20 feet above the current level of the lake. The cave is a water-cut cave, created around 4,000 years ago. This level would indicate that water levels were much higher at one time. In the 1970s, Fayette State Park gained jurisdiction over the site. At first, there was no communication, with local indigenous communities, concerning the preservation of this area. Spider Cave was listed on the National Register of Historic Places in 1971.

At one time, there were at least 13 pictographs at this site. Reportedly, 4 were inside the cave, and the rest were along the cliff face. In the 1960s the Lang family owned the land above the bluff. They built a set of stairs up to the cave and conducted a very successful tourism destination for many years. It was at that time that the site was surveyed, and the caves were excavated. One cave reportedly contained burials, another contained hundreds of projectile points. At that point in time, the images were clearly visible.

By 1995, things had changed dramatically. By then, only 4 of the images were still visible, and all of them were badly faded. The deterioration of the images was the result of several factors. Unfortunately, fame brought visitors and visitors cause damage. Images were dampened to make them more visible. People touched them and, walking about, kicked up dust, that clung to the pictures. Natural processes, like the growth of molds, also damaged the images. Even though the damage was known to the state, no measures were instituted to preserve these unique works of art. During a survey in 2016, we could only locate 3 drawings, all are in very bad condition. I would guess that, within a few years, they will be impossible to find unless you know exactly where to look.

There have been all kinds of interpretations of the meaning of these images. Some are pretty fanciful. If you consult the traditions of the Ojibway you find these explanations. The "spider man" pictograph is a representation of Mide. The circles beneath the torso represent the circles of our lives. They indicate the many pathways we can choose during our life journey. The "big man" pictograph depicts *Bug-way'ji-nini,* the Sacred Protector of the Forest. He is a guardian of this sacred site. The deterioration of these images, and the desecration of this sacred site is egregious. A precious treasure has been wasted and an historic site lost.

A Bit Of History: The first, and at the time, only toll road in Michigan was at Burnt Bluff. There was a white gate at Raymond's farm, which was located at the top of the bluff. After paying the toll, visitors drove down the rough road on a 250 drop over half a mile to the waters edge. The toll due was .25 per vehicle. Back in 1938, there was a dock and cottages at the lower end of the road. Today, there are a few cabins and a campground on the lake shore.

CARDIFF GIANT

Sometime in 1869, a farmer in upstate New York, hired workmen to help him dig a well. After working on the dig for a while, the workmen struck something solid buried, in the earth. The farmer asked them to remove the obstruction, since this was where he wanted his water well. After several hours of work around the object, the laborers revealed a giant. More work was required before a 10 foot tall, 3,000 pound, petrified giant human, was excavated from the earth. The news spread like wildfire. These were God fearing people, who read in their bible that in ancient times, "there were giants in the earth in those days", and now, a petrified giant had been found. The actual facts of the discovery of the giant, scientific opinion, and many subsequent events, are very much in dispute. Here is one account, compiled from reporting from that era.

Scientists and clergymen were summoned to view the giant, "in situ", so the historic discovery could be documented. Word had spread, and in a very short time, people from all over, were traveling to the farm to see the giant. Among the throngs was a famous man, with an idea, P.T. Barnum. He was convinced that the giant would be a fantastic addition to his "Greatest Show On Earth". He made the farmer a handsome offer and guaranteed that the giant would have a prominent place in the museum in New York. The farmer firmly declined the offer. He had seen the crowds of people lining up to see this wonder of the ages and he too had plans. He intended to take the giant on the road and tour the great cities of the east cost, charging for admission, of course.

That didn't stop old P.T. He hadn't become a great entrepreneur by being held up by such a simple obstacle. He acquired a large slab of granite and hired a sculptor to carve a copy of the "Cardiff Giant". Then he had the carving rolled in black dirt, they poured acid on the statue and set it on fire. All of this attention gave the new giant character, and a nicely aged patina. P.T. Barnum loaded his treasure on a wagon, sent his advance people out, and headed to the mid-west to wow the folks in the small towns there. His tour was very successful, as was, the tour of the real giant heading south along the Atlantic coast. Eventually, coastal towns ran out so the original headed west. P.T. Barnum and his tour ran out of towns west and decided to circle back to the southeast.

From this point, facts get murky, as several things happen in a short period of time. The chemical tests on the original "Cardiff Giant" had been completed and it was determined that the whole thing was a hoax. The farmer had had the giant sculpted and then buried it for a year so it could age. Then directed the laborers to dig at a specific spot so it could be "discovered". However, this was in an age of slow communications, so the disclosure didn't catch up with the road show for some time. Then, it happened that the original show, and the P.T. Barnum show, were approaching the same town on the same day. The farmer wasn't happy because he knew that the Barnum show had much better advance people and would probably get most of the business. Through various machinations, the farmer managed to get a local judge to issue an injunction that prevented P.T. Barnum from exhibiting his fake of the farmers hoax. Even that didn't stop old P.T. He rolled on through town, went to the Atlantic coast, loaded his giant on a ship, and toured Europe very profitably before the news of the whole thing caught up with him.

Now, I am not sure exactly where the original Cardiff Giant has ended up. It is somewhere in New York. The copy made by P.T. Barnum, however, is right here in Michigan. It is housed in Farmington Hills at Marvelous Marvin's Mechanical Museum. Marvelous Marvin's is easily one of the most unique museums anywhere in Michigan. It contains artifacts from many of the greatest magicians who ever lived including Alexander, Thurston, and Houdini.

The museum is actually a palace of entertainment. On over 5,000 square feet of floor space are hundreds of exhibits and old midway style games. You can play tic tac toe with an alien, have your fortune told, test your strength and get electrocuted. A favorite with the ladies is the "Love Shack". Here, a bearded, cigar smoking, foul mouthed midget tells you what your romantic prospects are in the future. There are games from every era and it is all hands on. Admission is free, making this a great place to take the kids. While you are having fun playing with all the games, don't forget a selfie with the giant. The fake, created by P.T. Barnum, is in a corner in the back, near the snack stand. Marvelous Marvin's is located at 31005 Orchard Lake Rd. Farmington Hills, Michigan.

BEAVER

ISLAND

IS

THE

LARGEST

ISLAND

IN

THAT

ARCHIPELAGO

IN

LAKE

MICHIGAN

CIRCLE OF STONES

Beaver Island, America's Emerald Isle, lies in Lake Michigan 37 miles off the mainland, in Charlevoix County. Beaver is the largest island in an archipelago that has been home to many peoples. The Irish came here. In fact, many road signs on the island are still in Gaelic. The Mormon's came and established a monarchy, with King Strang as their leader. Long before either of those, these islands were occupied by Native Americans. The importance of these islands, as part of trade and migration routes, can't be overstated. Ancient peoples left traces of their presence like bent trees as way markers, extensive gardens, and the circle of stones.

The enigmatic circle is on the west side of Beaver Island, below Angeline's Bluff . These are not towering standing stones, like Great Britain's Stonehenge. This monolithic construction, consists of a circle of glacial boulders, that is nearly 400' feet across. The undergrowth and dense forest make it difficult to get an idea of how big this circle is. The center stone has a hole apparently bored or carved into it. The hole suggests that a pole could be inserted. Calling this a circle is a bit misleading. There are actually remnants of concentric circles within the construction. There also appears to be evidence of straight lines leading out from the center, or "spokes". Several of these stones have markings that have been interpreted as an ancient script or rock faces. One "face rock" is located at the museum downtown.

The circle of stones was forgotten, and then was rediscovered in the 1980s. The layout of the circle of stones is reminiscent of a stone calendar. Native American elders tell of old tribal stories about a "medicine wheel of life" circle. Archaeologist, M.T. Bussey, has done extensive work to uncover and interpret the meaning of the circle. Her survey seems to indicate astronomical alignments in the layout of the stones. There is an excellent sketch of the layout on her website. The circle of stones is real. Research continues to determine the age and origin of this megalithic site.

There are other mysteries to explore. Ancient gardens were mentioned in King Strang's writings.

Evidence of such gardens has been found near the airport. Then there is the report of a discovery beneath the waters of Lake Michigan. Just a few miles offshore is what may be an underwater Stonehenge-like structure. Forty feet beneath the waters of Lake Michigan, this enigmatic circle consists of standing stones, which seem to bear carvings. One particular carving appears to be a mastodon. If the carvings prove authentic, the structure is man-made. Research is being conducted on the site, sporadically. The underwater location makes up close, scientific inspection, difficult.

Directions: To find the circle of stones, contact the historical society. REMEMBER, do not disturb the stones. This is a precious construction from the past, and may very well be a sacred site, as well.

THE

CORNISH

PUMP

WAS

THE

LARGEST

OF

IT'S

KIND

CONSTRUCTED

IN

AMERICA

CORNISH PUMP

The exploration and settlement of the Western Upper Peninsula of Michigan was driven by the lumber industry, as well as, the quest for copper and iron. The Menominee Range contained numerous iron mines, several of which were discovered around the "iron mountain" on the Wisconsin border. The Chapin Mine was to become the most productive. In fact, it would become one of the greatest iron mines in the world. The town of Iron Mountain began in 1879 due to the great wealth of the Chapin Mine.

As the mine was developed it was discovered that part of the ore was underneath a cedar swamp. Water seeping into the mine shafts became an ever increasing problem, causing a number of accidents. Ground based pumps were installed to remove the constant accumulation of seeping water. This solution handled the problem for many years, but as the miners dug deeper into the earth, the ground pumps were overwhelmed. A new solution was needed. That solution was found in the tin mines of Cornwall where miners had been dealing with wet mines for generations.

A new pump was designed to handle the unique conditions in the mine. The steam-driven engine developed became known as the "Cornish Pump". The pump was and is gigantic. The pump weighs in at 160 tons and is 54 feet tall. The flywheel alone is 40 feet in diameter. In fact, part of the flywheel turns in a trench beneath ground level. It is still the largest reciprocating steam-driven engine ever built in the United States. This enormous pump kept the mine dry enough for mining operations for years. The Chapin Mine eventually produced over 27 million tons of iron ore.

The mine closed in 1932 and the Cornish Pump was donated to Dickinson County. It is currently on display in the Cornish Pump Museum. No written description can prepare the visitor for the first time you see this machine. The size of the pump simply overwhelms. While there are lots of other exhibits in many museums across the Upper Peninsula, the Cornish Pump literally towers over all of them.

EBEN ICE CAVES

The Rock River Canyon Ice Caves, also known as the Eben Ice Caves, are a unique destination, for a winter day trip. While this beautiful natural wonder, is being visited more often, many people, have still never heard of it. The Rock River Wilderness, in the upper peninsula of Michigan, includes over 4,000 acres, in the Hiawatha National Forest. The ice caves, are high up on the wall, of the river gorge, with ice formations as much as sixty feet tall. These giant sheets of ice are formed by water seeping through the rock wall. As the water flows down the rock wall, it freezes into beautiful curtains of ice. Eventually, the ice reaches the the bottom of the wall. The ice conceals undercuts in the cliff face, which become ice caves.

This spot would be worth visiting, just to see the frozen wall of ice, but the fact that you can go into the caves, formed by the cascades of ice, make this a one-of-a-kind destination. The caves are large enough that you can walk around inside. The interior is well lit by daylight filtering through the translucent ice wall. Stalactites of ice will be hanging from the ceiling. There are even windows, formed naturally, that afford a view of the pristine forest outside the caves.

The sheets of ice that form the great wall can be three feet thick or more and are very strong. Some people come specifically, to climb the ice walls. Even if you are not an ice climber, there is a rope, at one end of the cliff, that can be used to get to the top. From up there, you can get a panoramic view of the entire ice formation, the forest, and the river gorge.

When you arrive at the parking area, you will find minimal facilities, so take your water and energy bars with you. In fact, on a week day, you may be the only people there. The trail or pathway is easy to follow, as the snow will be well packed down by other hikers. The first part of the hike, crosses a farm field, to the treeline. The second part, is pretty easy as well, through a quiet woodlands, toward the river gorge. About half way to the river, you will come to a sign describing the area, and pointing out that, the trail into the gorge is steep, slippery, and possibly treacherous; believe it.

The final part of the hike is into the gorge, with steep up and down sections. Not only is it slippery, and treacherous going down to the river, it is just as wild, when you climb back up. The trail is snow covered, with wet rocks, and icy conditions. There are a couple of spots, where small streams and crevasses, must be crossed. Cleats on hiking boots, come in very handy, in some sections of the trail. When you reach the river, at the bottom of the gorge, you still have a short hike, along the waterway. Then, you will have a short, steep climb, up to the caves. The hike is over a mile, all told, but the caves make it worth every bit of effort. The giant ice formation, looks like a frozen waterfall. You can actually walk, inside the cavern, and experience the light, coming through a curtain of ice.

Directions: The caves are just outside Eben Junction, on Route 94, in the Upper Peninsula. Follow Route 94 west out of Munising, until you get to Eben Junction. Follow the small yellow signs, to the ice caves.

REPORTS

OF

THE

GLOWING

TOMBSTONES

DATE

FROM

BEFORE

AUTOMOBILES

AND

ARTIFICIAL

LIGHTS

GLOWING TOMBSTONES

Beginning in the late 1800s, the locals around Evart, Michigan began hearing of strange doings in the Forest Hill Cemetery. People were whispering about a light moving through the distance. Tales were told of eerie light in the cemetery on moonless nights. Some said that the tombstones themselves were glowing in the dark.

A few courageous souls ventured into the cemetery, trying to discover the source of the light. They reported that the tombstones did seem to be glowing with a reflected light. A glow, from an unseen light, appeared to move from grave to grave, reflecting off each headstone. Though they searched through the night, no source for the light could be found.

Reports of the "glowing tombstone" phenomena, appeared in newspapers of the day. This was at a time when there were no automobile headlights, and no light pollution from night mercury lights, it was a time when the night was dark. From time to time, another traveler would report glowing tombstones, visible from the road. There are still reports to this day of a strange glow among the graves.

Old timers say the first reports began after a young boy fell from a train. An Italian railroad worker had taken his son along on a run. At the end of the line the, the boy was missing. They say the ghost of the railroad man searches for his son. The light is from his lantern, as he reads the headstones, searching for his sons name.

GRAVITY MYSTERY – BENZONIA

Up in the far northwest, of the lower peninsula of Michigan, is the famous Sleeping Bear Dunes National Lakeshore. When you have had enough of tubing the river and drinking in the glorious sunsets, you might want to take a short side trip, to the southeast section Benzie County. The easiest way to get there is to take Hwy. 22 south out of Frankfort. Many hundreds of people make this drive every year, to experience a spot where gravity seems to go haywire. You can take either Hwy. 22 or Hwy. 31. Turn onto Joyfield Road. and travel along until you get to Putney Road. On that corner you will see an old church that is more than 110 years old. It is the only building that remains of the community that once was here. Turn south at the church onto Putney Road. Drive downhill about fifty yards past the church. There will be pine trees just ahead on your right.

Stop your car, keep your foot firmly on the brake, and shift the car into neutral. Be prepared for a surprise. When you take your foot off the brake, your car will immediately start going backwards up the hill, and it will be going quickly enough to startle you, so be ready. You can go down to the curve, turn around and try it going forward. The effect is quite remarkable. Your car will start moving almost immediately, and will move much faster than you would think. Call it an optical illusion or haywire gravity, the effect is real and it's lots of fun.

Along The Way: Just a bit further south, on Highway 22, is the Lake Michigan Overlook. This is one of the highest spots anywhere on Lake Michigan. The view from there is well worth it.

All of this running around might work up an appetite. I always head for the Cabbage Shed, in Elberta, just south of Frankfort. They know how to build a Guinness and the food is always delicious. They make the best borscht I have ever had.

A Bit Of History: The locals have known about this spot for decades, though there is no agreement on how it was first discovered. One story tells it that two young fellows took a couple of girls for a horse and buggy ride, back before there were automobiles. As luck would have it, there was some kind of problem with the harness and when they unhooked the horses, to fix things up, the buggy backed up the hill and into the ditch. The story doesn't include how the boys explained why they were out in such a secluded spot with these innocent girls, instead of being in the fields working, where they were supposed to be.

THE

LOOP

HARRISON

MANSION

IS

PART

OF

THE

SANILAC

COUNTY

HISTORICAL

MUSEUM

HAUNTED MANSION

About half way up the "thumb" of Michigan is Port Sanilac, originally known as Bark Shanty. This small village is home to multiple treasures, including the Loop-Harrison Mansion, on the grounds of the Sanilac County Historical Museum. For years there have been tales of strange encounters in the Mansion. There have been unexplained aromas, voices, apparitions, music, and furniture moving about.

Ada Loop-Harrison had died tragically in front of the mansion in an automobile accident in 1925. Since that time, her apparition has been seen walking the beach, at nearby Lake Huron. When the mansion is decorated for the Christmas season, visitors often ask who is playing the music upstairs.   The volunteers at the museum usually say, "it must be Ada", because there isn't anyone upstairs. Professional paranormal researchers have established that there is a "presence", most likely benevolent.

The mansion is the main building, in what has now grown into an historic village, containing a railroad depot, general store, church, log cabins, and much more. In addition, the complex includes one of the few operating Barn Theaters left in Michigan. The museum grounds are the site of a number of festivals throughout the year including an excellent wine tasting event. The mansion remains the main attraction, and is open for tours during the season. It is also decorated and open during the Christmas season.

Directions: Port Sanilac is only about an hour north of Detroit using I-94 to Route 25. From Lansing use I-69 to 25 and from Saginaw, just take a back roads drive on Route 46 right into town.

HEART OF LA BRANCHE

Several years ago, a Menominee County group was mining aggregate, near the town of La Branche, in the upper peninsula. Gravel was dug with giant shovels and dumped onto conveyor belts, to be moved to the sorting operations. On one particular day, the conveyor that moved the gravel, suddenly ground to a halt. The operator quickly shut things down to prevent damage. Upon investigation, they discovered a large stone, jammed into the machine. After the men managed to wrestle the rock out of the machinery, they realized they had dug up something quite unusual.

The rock, which became known as the "Heart of La Branche", actually is in the shape of a heart. It is about the same size as a 12 pack of soda. The object is quite smooth, almost like a river rock, that has been smoothed by the action of water and sand. Another unusual property is revealed, if you whack it with a hammer. The sound produced is very similar to the sound made when hitting an anvil. Then there is the weight. This relatively small rock weighs in at more than 240 pounds. Finally, it seems to be faintly magnetic. I am not aware of any assay tests having been done, so don't know what the "Heart" is composed of. No one really has any idea how this was formed, or what it was doing in a common gravel pit.

The rock caused a brief sensation. After a brief time of showing the unusual rock around, it was time to get back to work. The "Heart" was tossed aside. This oddity was nearly lost. The gravel pit operators thought of selling it off for scrap, but never got around to it. It was pretty much forgotten about. After gravel operations were shut down someone remembered the strange stone, and decided to call George Potvin, to see if he wanted it.

George was the right man to call, he knows metal. He operates the Ten Mile Creek Forge and is an internationally recognized knife maker. George conducts one-on-one classes, teaching the fundamental techniques of blacksmithing from tending the forge, all the way to cutting, bending, and finishing. In addition to the forge, he and his wife operate a gift shop on the same property. The shop at the Ten Mile Creek Forge is described as a pottery and lighting gift shop. It actually holds original work by about 30 juried artists. It is also home to the "Heart of La Branche". Between the shop and the forge, a short drive out of Escanaba to see the "Heart" is a scenic day trip.

Directions: The Ten Mile Creek Forge has a Bark River address. Follow the signs between Gladstone and Escanaba or go to Bark River and follow the signs from there.

THE

LANGLEY

BRIDGE

IS

THE

LONGEST

COVERED

BRIDGE

IN

MICHIGAN

HIDDEN TREASURES – ROUTE 60

There are a couple of real treasures along Route 60 west of I-69. These are interesting spots to visit and there is unique history. Route 60 is found off I-69 south of Battle Creek. It is one of the old stage coach routes that ran between Jackson and Three Rivers.

The first stop is the Burlington Store. Burlington is a tiny town just a few miles west of the busy Interstate Highway. It is so small that even Route 60 bypasses the town. If you don't take the side road into town, you will miss the treasure at the Burlington Store. The town is really small and little traffic passes through. Being off the beaten path, the Burlington Store is often only open on Friday, and weekends.

So, you pull up, have a look at the Burlington Store, and the first reaction you may have is that the author has a screw loose. The store, from the outside, looks like just another craft store in a small town. That impression is reinforced when you go inside. This is an old, small town hardware store that has become half hardware, and half arts and crafts. The hardware side is worth a look. There are old items here that most people can't even identify. The crafts side is cool too, lots of country crafts on display. The treasure is on the second floor.

Ask the owner if you can go upstairs to see the doll museum, it is amazing. You go outside and around to a side door. That leads to a stairway up to the second floor. As soon as you get to the upper floor, there are the dolls; thousands of them. The entire second floor has dolls on display. Many of the dolls are in their original packaging. Cabbage Patch Kids, GI Joe, Barbie, and even Betty Boop are here. In addition, to the dolls are the doll houses. A couple of those are big enough for small children to play inside. It is difficult to describe the smiles and laughter that break out in this room from all the girls of all ages. There is no charge to visit the museum, but you will have to ask to gain entrance.

Rawson's King Mill is just north of Route 60, east of Mendon and west of Burlington. The King Mill is one of the last remaining vertical shaft gristmills in the United States. The current building was constructed in the early 1870s and is reported to have produced more than 1,000 barrels of flour in 1873. In 1843 the first "flour ark" left the mill, and headed downstream toward Three Rivers where the flour was trans-shipped to Chicago and points west. By the 1960s the mill was processing more than 25,000 barrels of wheat, but then regulations shut the mill down once again. Today this mill is not in production, but is still in operating condition. The mill and surrounding grounds are part of a county park. There are quiet waterways, walking paths, and picnic areas, beautiful.

Just a few miles west on Route 60 is Mendon, Michigan. The old Wakeman House building is still there. Also known as the Mendon County Inn, this is the site of one of the most remarkable events in Michigan history. The Wakeman House had been here for more than a hundred years. It served as an important stop for stage coaches traveling through the wilderness of Michigan. There are many stories about things that happened here. My favorite involves a late night poker game, and the story of "Lady Godiva" in Michigan.

It seems that a stage coach had stopped to change horses. Here the passengers could take a break from the rough ride on the old dirt trail that served as a road. During this break, one of those huge thunderstorms for which Michigan is famous, blew in, dropped inches of rain, and turned the road into a quagmire. The stagecoach wasn't going to move for some hours due to road conditions. At the same time, a young lady of a well known local family, was out exercising one of her horses. She was a skilled equestrian and it wasn't unusual for her to be riding alone. She was caught in the storm and also took shelter at the inn.

The stagecoach passengers were also caught by the storm. As darkness fell, they decided to play a little poker. The equestrian was a good player and she joined in the game. Late at night the game took an unfortunate turn. The details are a bit sketchy. The story goes that the lady made a bet that one of the other players didn't like, and a row ensued. She finally convinced him to take the bet, but he insisted that if she lost, she had to ride through town clothed only in her natural glory. She took the bet, lost, and kept her word. She rode through town wearing nothing but a smile, on two horses, and then rode them right into the poker room at the Inn to prove she had paid off her bet. With a bit of digging, you can discover the names of the people involved in this event.

If you keep going west out of Mendon, you will come to a sign directing you to Centreville. That road will take you to the Langley Covered Bridge, the longest covered bridge in Michigan.

Directions: The Burlington Store is easy to find. It is the only store in downtown Burlington. Rawson's King Mill - Take Zinmaster Road north and follow the curve around, go all the way to the dead end. Go left and as you enter an area with lots of trees you will find the park. The last time I went, some of the roadways were gravel. Mendon, Michigan, and the Wakeman House are on Route 60 west of Burlington.

THE

HOLES

IN

THE

WOODS

ARE

ALL

IDENTICAL

IN

SIZE

AND

DEPTH

HOLES IN THE WOODS

Sometimes we find evidence of past constructions that are enigmatic. One example are the holes in the forest up in Delta County in the upper peninsula. While not particularly bizarre, the holes are difficult to explain. The holes are found in the forest some distance from a river and a couple of hundred yards from the nearest road. The holes are laid out in a very well defined grid pattern.

This area has heavy undergrowth making the search very difficult. We actually found the first two holes by stepping into them. Once we understood that there was a pattern, we quickly found several more holes. We identified a grid at least 40' x 30' with the holes being consistently 10' apart. It is entirely possible that the grid is much larger. The holes are very consistent, about 12" across and 6" deep, the sides and bottom are lined with stones. There is no wood in the holes and no posts of any kind.

In addition, there is a large rock inside the grid. It has a rectangular cut out in the top of it. I have seen this formation before and understand that it was used to sharpen stakes. There is no way to determine if the large stone and the holes came to be here at the same time.

These holes pose a number of problems. While they are located in a remote, densely forested area, it is an area that has been regularly occupied. The family living there now has been there for several generations. Yet, there are no family stories about the existence of the holes, or their purpose. At 6 inches, they aren't deep enough to serve as foundation holes for a pole barn, lodge, or any other tall construction. Still, they are there, they are obviously man-made, and they are well constructed.

One possible clue, is that there is a nearby river, and Lake Michigan is only a short distance away. It may be that a game or fish drying rack was constructed at this spot. Native Americans have lived here for hundreds of years and this is quite close to the sacred site at Burnt Bluffs. Short posts could be stood up in these holes. Those posts could be bound together with a low mesh of branches upon which game could be hung for drying or smoking. This is just speculation, but it is one reasonable explanation, such constructions were common. Another grid of holes had been found a few yards away, but we were unable to locate it.

The family tells of a strange incident that happened to their grandfather on this homestead. The story goes that grandpa was working in the forest when he found a large, painted, pottery pot. It was quite beautiful, so he decided to take it home.

That very night grandpa had a disturbing dream. He told the family next morning that an Indian had been standing over him. The Indian was pointing his finger in an admonishing manner, and saying something over and over, in a language that grandpa didn't understand. Grandpa experienced the same dream the next night. He had the dream again on the third night, and each night, the Indian seemed even more agitated. The dream was so disturbing and frightening that on the fourth day, he took the pot back into the forest and left it there. After returning the pot to the forest, he never had the dream again.

There was a lot of interaction between Europeans and Native Americans. The family tells how in the 1870s, Indian George was almost part of the family, teaching the children about the natural world around them. His last name was either Sigasaw or Sigataw. He was Pottawattami and a medicine man. Those who were ill in nearby tribes traveled here for healing. Those who died were buried nearby. Indian George buried his family here after a tragic turn of events. He had traveled to another community to tend to the sick. While he was away, his entire family died after contracting measles. Sadly, the healer wasn't on hand to help his own people.

HUMONGOUS FUNGUS

Small golden button mushrooms, growing up through a tree stump, turn out to be just the tip of the proverbial iceberg. In 1988, in the forest near Crystal Falls, Michigan, they discovered a giant organism, Armillaria bulbosa. The small honey mushrooms, peaking up through the forest floor, turned out to be part of an enormous fungus. At that time, it was believed to be the largest and oldest living organism on earth. When I say giant I mean it, the humongous fungus covers 37 acres at last measurement. It is estimated that, if you could pull the whole thing up, it would weigh more than 100 tons. Since then other giant mushrooms have been found. One, in Oregon, is said to cover more than 2,000 acres.

The residents of Crystal Falls are still celebrating the discovery of "Humongous". Whether theirs is the biggest or not hasn't stopped the celebration, the show must go on. Every August for three days, it is "all things mushroom" during the Humongous Fungus Festival. Each day starts with a pancake breakfast. After that revelers can tube down the Paint River, or enter a cribbage tournament. There are softball, golf, volleyball and horseshoe tournaments. Hungry festival goers can compete in the pie eating contests and ice cream socials, while enjoying the craft show, fireworks, and the Fungus Fest Parade. All of this leads up to the main event, baking, and eating the Humongous Pizza.
The folks in Crystal Falls are darned proud of this pizza.

Producing the largest pizza in the world is an annual, world-wide, competition. The Humongous Pizza, measuring 10 feet by 10 feet, is the largest mushroom pizza in the world. Made with honey mushrooms from the huge fungus in the forest, the entire pizza is consumed every year.

Crystal Falls is in Iron County in the upper peninsula, a few miles north of the Split Rock. The festival activities take place all over town. One of the main check in spots, is Runkle Park, on the east side of town. Several of the events take place in the park and it is a great place for camping.

IDLEWILD REVISITED

In Lake County, Michigan, is a small town with a most unique history. Idlewild enjoyed explosive growth and popularity, nearly became a ghost town, and is on the rise again. This was the first free black community in Michigan. At its peak, Idlewild had become the premier resort destination, for African Americans in the midwest. The town was built by and for African Americans, and every possible amenity was at hand. In the 1920's, this town became home for the black middle class and a destination for everyone. In the summer season the population would grow to 3,000+. From the 1920's through the 1940's, Idlewild hosted the biggest names in entertainment. The famous performers at the theater included Calloway, Ellington, Armstrong and Hampton. There was another resident who shouldn't be forgotten. Dr. Daniel Williams lived here. He was the first person to operate on a human heart.

What You'll Find: Driving through the old part of Idlewild can give you a sense of the hope and inspiration that was here, just by the street names.

Most of the old homes are abandoned now, the original downtown is pretty much empty. The bathhouse and the famous 60 room hotel that were on the island in the lake are gone as well. However, there are signs of renewed interest and growth. A new community center has opened, and the museum is welcoming visitors. Each year the Idlewild Music Festival celebrates the history that was made here.

Directions: Idlewild is on Route 10 just a few miles east of Baldwin.

Side Trips: A day trip to the area should include a visit to the famous Jones Ice Cream, in Baldwin. Generations of visitors to the area say it is the best ice cream in Michigan. Right across the street is Pandora's Box where all kinds of Michigan made items are available. Just south of Bitely is the Loda Wildflower Sanctuary, one of only a few in America. On the south edge of Baldwin is the Shrine of the Pines museum. Their exhibits include the largest collection of white pine rustic furniture in the world.

THE KEWEENAW WALL

Near the historic town of Laurium, on the Keweenaw Peninsula, there is an enigmatic wall. The huge stone wall is in a deep ravine, is considered by some to be man-made, and has been the subject of debate for generations. Early photographs, from one angle, suggested that the "wall" showed the profile of a Native American.

The wall appears to be constructed of large, squared blocks of stone. The horizontal seams between blocks run very straight and the vertical are staggered giving the whole thing the appearance of a block wall with courses, just like you would see in a brick or concrete block wall. Each block of stone is a couple of feet thick and three to four feet long.

The ravine is deep. I would estimate it at roughly 60 feet in depth. The sides of the gorge are extremely steep. The wall itself is partially broken, but the intact portion protrudes out of the side of the ravine on one side. On the opposite side only parts of the wall remain, forming a sort of stairway that is a real help in climbing down and back up. The remnant of the wall that is still intact is at least 30 feet tall. There are fragments of the wall scattered about the small stream that runs through the bottom of the ravine. The presence of that stream has led to speculation that the wall was built as a dam to create a lake or watering hole.

In spite of the "stairs" formed by wall blocks on one side of the ravine, the way down is treacherous. It is steep and slippery. There are no railings, no ropes, and no cell service. In other words, a trek into this ravine is no joke and, you will have to climb back up out without aid. It is only from the bottom that you can fully appreciate the enormity of this object, but it is probably a bad idea to go down into the ravine alone. One slip and it is a long fall. However, you can get a good look at the wall without going into the ravine.

The ravine and the wall are on private property, so I am not giving directions. However, this anomaly has been known for a long time so an internet search will provide the exact location.

There is another rarity in this neck of the woods.

Just a couple miles away is a patch of open bedrock that is covered with glacial scratches or grooves. This patch of bare bedrock is about the size of a small room. Deep grooves, from four feet long to about twelve, are carved into the rock. The grooves are several inches wide and a few inches deep. These grooves were created by rocks in the bottom of glaciers. As the glacier receded the rocks carved the scratches into the softer bedrock. The bedrock and grooves have a sort of, polished appearance. This is the result of fine grains of sand, also embedded in the glacier, acting as a sanding or polishing agent. Interestingly, some grooves run about south to north and some run west to east. This is unexpected because we think of the glaciers in terms of receding south to north as the climate began to warm at the end of the last ice age. The explanation is simple according to one source. It seems that at this spot, three different glaciers were present and, as they receded, they banged into each other causing at least one of them to move west to east for a period of time.

The glacial groove formation is found behind the Calumet high school a bit east of the parking lot near the soccer field. Just look for bare rock in the otherwise grassy area.

LAVENDER LABYRINTH

Labyrinths are found around the world. They have been constructed since ancient times. Unlike a maze, a labyrinth is a continuous circuit, and you cannot get lost. Pilgrims entering the great cathedrals of France, during the middle ages, walked the labyrinths inlaid in the cathedral floor. The slow walk was to prepare them, for the sacred experience they were about to participate in. There is a truly beautiful labyrinth right here in Michigan.

The Lavender Labyrinth is in the area of Oceana County known as Little Point Sable. World famous as a destination for sun and sand, this area is also home to rich farm lands and a long agricultural heritage. The labyrinth is on the grounds of Cherry Point Farm west of Hart. It is formed of living lavender and covers several acres. Enhanced by ornamental rocks, flower beds, and pergolas, it is a unique destination for a cool nature walk. The labyrinth, which takes about an hour to walk, is open to anyone: church groups, herb societies, drumming circles or individuals seeking new experiences.

There is no charge, and reservations are not needed. Even if you don't have the hour, it is worth taking a look just to enjoy the sheer beauty of the labyrinth. The Lavender Labyrinth is in full bloom in July and August. The farm includes a market that is famous for cherries, strudel and daily fish boils during the summer season.

Directions: The address is 9600 West Buchanan Road, Shelby, MI 49455

From Grand Haven/Muskegon go north on U.S. 31 to the Shelby exit head west. The scenic route from either Pentwater or Montague is Route B-15.

LIGNUM VITAE

Lignum Vitae is one of the oddest of the oddities in Michigan and certainly one of the rarest of the rarities. Lignum vitae is a type of wood. It is harvested from trees that grow in the Caribbean and the northern coast of South America. It has been an important export crop to Europe for hundreds of years and it has been essential to Sault Ste. Marie since the early 1900s. Without this unusual wood, the Cloverland Hydroelectric Plant with 74 high speed turbines handling a water flow of 28,000 feet per second, might not have been built. The plant was used to produce electricity for Union Carbide. In 1963 Edison Sault acquired the plant and, today, it serves over 40,000 urban and rural customers. Lignum Vitae was an essential component in the construction of the plant and the production of electricity.

Lignum Vitae is extremely dense, so dense in fact, that it will not float. A cube that is 12 inches square weighs between 25 and 30 pounds. Besides density, lignum vitae has other characteristics that made it ideal for use as bearings for those high speed turbines. The natural oils in the wood have lubricating properties that create a film between the wood and the metal shaft about 2 to 3 thousandths of an inch thick. Turns out that is just about perfect for spinning turbine shafts. Another effect of this film of oil is that you can stop the turbine and leave it in rest for extended periods of time without danger of corrosion. Such a rest stop isn't possible with metal bearings. Each turbine requires a main bearing and 3 steadying bearings 120 degrees apart. In the old days, logs of lignum vitae were kept at the electric plant, submerged in water. When a bearing wore out and had to be replaced, a log was brought up and a coin cut from the end. The log was then submerged again. The coin would be taken into the shop for machining.

At this writing some bearings made of lignum vitae are still used at the plant. The oldest has been in service for more than 60 years. The trees that produce this rare wood are now farmed. It remains in demand because some places have water that has high acidity unlike the pure waters of Lake Superior. Acidic waters cause rapid corrosion which plays havoc with metal bearings. You can check out the turbines and Lignum Vitae one day each year during the Engineers Day Festival in Sault Ste. Marie. On that day only the interior the Cloverland Hydroelectric Plant is open to visitors.

LIGNUM

VITAE

IS

ALSO

USED

FOR

BOAT

GEARS

MACINTOSH STONE

There are mysteries in Michigan's history, people who disappeared, unexplained artifacts, even forgotten cultures. One of those mysteries has to do with the tons of copper that were extracted from thousands of prehistoric mines on Isle Royale and the Keweenaw Peninsula. Some surveys recognize more than 3,000 prehistoric mines on Isle Royale alone. Researchers say up to 500,000 tons of nearly pure copper was removed before Europeans arrived in the 1500s. The mystery is that all that copper is missing from the archeological record in North America. The ancient mines are there, but the copper is missing. It should be easy to locate because it is easy to identify. This was Michigan float copper. So, the chemical composition is well known, and unique to the Lake Superior area.

The speculations about the Great Lakes copper have been covered in many books and articles. The subject has even been covered in an episode or two of the television program America Unearthed. The theory is that mariners made their way to North America thousands of years ago to mine copper to supply demand in the ancient world during the Bronze age. Since smelting technology wasn't needed for this pure copper, it was readily available to ancient peoples. It supposed that these seafarers were Egyptian, Phoenician, Chinese, or even Vikings. There is plenty of evidence that copper was widely traded in the Old World. The speculation focuses on the source for all that copper. Sometimes rumors would surface about evidence of visitors to the Great Lakes by pre-columbian miners. Usually the "evidence" would prove to be a hoax, unverified or would simply disappear. However, there are two objects in existence that may support the idea that ancient mariners did make it to the Keweenaw Peninsula. One is known as the MacIntosh Stone.

In the mid-1980s, Charley Macintosh was out doing his job, surveying timber, far up on the Keweenaw Peninsula. This work took him to remote locations, so break time was spent in the wilderness. Charley took up the hobby of picking agates on the shore of Lake Superior during his free time. Agates don't look like much until cleaned and polished. After that process, the real beauty of agates is revealed. On the day the stone was found, Charley was on the shore about 8 miles east of Copper Harbor. Manitou Island was visible in the distance. Isle Royale lay to the north, nearly 50 miles away. Charley was working an excellent field of stones about 50 feet above the waterline. As usual, he picked up likely looking specimens, and put them in a bag. Back home, he went about cleaning debris from the stones in preparation for polishing. One stone, when washed, proved to be covered with odd engravings.

The MacIntosh Stone is small, about the size of two dimes laid side by side. It is amazing that it was ever found at all, amid a million stones of the same size. The stone has a dark coloration, is almond shaped and has a whitish vein running through it. It is completely covered with engravings. Photographs of the stone were published in the book "Coming for Copper" by researchers from the Ancient Artifact Preservation Society. The book offered almost no information about the origin of the object, what culture produced it and what tool could have been used to create these intricate carvings on such a small object.

Early speculations about the stone were usually conducted after consulting the photographs only. A few researchers examined the stone in person, but most depended on the images. Looking at the original pictures didn't reveal much. There definitely are images, set in frames, almost like cartouches. Cartouches are best known from Egyptian hieroglyphs, so some people thought this object could be of Eastern Mediterranean origin. The cameo, or cartouche, style of carving just added to the mystery. Cartouche or not, the carvings within those frames are just as puzzling. Some images have been interpreted as a bird, a bear, and a crescent moon. Other observers saw, worship symbols, Celtic shamanic symbols or Native American totems. The purpose of the stone was also unknown. Some thought it was a Phoenician prayer stone carried by illiterate sailors to remind them to say their prayers at the appropriate times. Some said the stone was a Native American totem, possibly Hopewell, and would be carried in a Medicine Bag. It may have had a bezel so it could be worn as a necklace. According to Dr. Robert Duff, who examined photos of this stone, that veining is an important element in determining authenticity.

Even after another round of examinations by the experts in 2017, there wasn't much progress except the idea that the crescent moon might be a boat. When viewed from the correct angle, that seemed a viable idea. Then a series of chance events revealed the meaning of several of the carvings. A casual conversation while looking at pictures of the stone led to the discovery that there are human figures on one side. In fact, the frame containing the spider turns out to show a seated person. In the next frame is another man, in a kneeling position, facing the seated man. Behind the kneeling figure is another smaller figure that appears to be kneeling as well. As a result of this discovery, I had a professional photographer produce high resolution images of all sides of the stone.

When those were completed the images of the people were quite clear. In addition, the possible boat on the opposite side became clear. Above the boat is a carving that remained a puzzle until another odd chance event. The carving looks like a bird head to some and a figure eight to others. Some people speculated that if it was a bird head, the combination with the boat could be seen as a bird sitting on a nest. The chance event was the discovery of a photograph of a petroglyph from the 13th century in the book "Bronze Age America" by Barry Fell. The photograph shows a double hulled ship very similar to the one on the MacIntosh Stone. In the same photo the figure eight symbol is shown. The figure eight is identified as buckler, bukla and a ring. There are also Tifinag letters in the picture. The combination of these symbols is translated as "thrust out (to sea) at launching". Amazingly, these same symbols appear on the shield of the Westford Knight.

The discovery of the bukla and ring in conjunction with the ship leant new meaning to the carvings of the men on the opposite side of the stone. If Fell's translation is correct, the stone may be a commemoration or blessing of a sea journey about to be undertaken by a knight and his squire. Another idea is that it could have been created as a charm for sea voyage. Whatever the meaning of carvings and however this artifact was created, it found its way to the Keweenaw Peninsula for Charley MacIntosh to find while picking agates. The stone is kept at the Nahma Inn in Nahma, Michigan. The images can be seen on the website www.michiganbackroads.com.

THE

MACINTOSH

STONE

IS

ABOUT

TWICE

THE

SIZE

OF

AN

ALMOND

MAGNETIC HEALING SPRINGS

It happened in St. Louis, Michigan, in 1869. A group of men were drilling a well, in hopes of tapping into an underground source of brine. The plan was to bring the water up and let it evaporate. The salt left behind could be sold. They did hit underground water, but it wasn't brine. In fact, they claim it was magnetic. Allegedly, metal objects dipped into the water, became magnetized. That wasn't all. One of the workmen suffered from arthritis in his hands. Within a couple of days of getting his hands wet in the new well water, he noticed significant relief, from the pain and swelling. The story of the apparent curative powers spread quickly, and within just a couple of years, St. Louis, Michigan became the destination for thousands of folks heading for the curative baths.

Celebrities were among those who hurried to Michigan including, General Hooker of Civil War fame, Allan Pinkerton, and Salmon P. Chase. Documented cures were so numerous, that at a time when most roads were mere trails, and railroads scarce, St. Louis received mail deliveries

24 times per week. There were churches, libraries, an opera house and first-class hotels. It is said that the incredible success of those magnetic springs, led to the "discovery" of healing springs, in several other towns around Michigan.

St. Louis is a small town in the "middle of the mitten". The spas and bathhouses are long gone, but there is still some beautiful architecture around town. The opera house has been converted and the magnetic well has been capped. The history of St. Louis, during the magnetic springs boom days is, full of amazing stories. The local historical society can provide some of the details from that unique time. The book "The Saratoga of the West" tells the whole story.

A Scenic Drive: If you are looking for a beautiful drive through mid-Michigan, St. Louis is a good place to start. Take Main Street north across the river and turn right on East Prospect. Go about three blocks and turn north again on Union Street. As you leave town this road becomes Riverside Drive and will lead you to the Pine River Road. For the next 20 miles the road winds through woodlands and farmlands and hugging the river most of the way. Toward the end of this drive is another scenic back road that will take you right into Midland.

Directions: St. Louis, Michigan is on Route 46 about an hour north of Lansing.

SENEY

IS

HALF

WAY

BETWEEN

LAKE

MICHIGAN

AND

LAKE

SUPERIOR

MICHIGAN'S BOOT HILL CEMETERY

Schoolcraft County is in the central part of the upper peninsula. Much of the county is still uninhabited. A large section is dedicated to the Seney wildlife preserve. On the eastern edge of the preserve is the town of Seney, and while most folks just roll through on their way somewhere else, there is great history in this tiny crossroads. Seney has an old cemetery that was known as Boot Hill. While it didn't become as famous as the one out west, it did become the final resting place of some of the famous and infamous. Many of those buried here were legendary characters, larger than life lumber men and adventurers, who lived during the great lumber days of the 1880s and the 1890s. Some were travelers, stranded here, who's identity has been lost.

During those rip-roaring years, this was one of the toughest and roughest towns in the world. Tales are told of the fights, robberies and killings that greeted the traveler. Characters like Leon Czolgosz, who later assassinated President McKinley and P.J. "Snap Jaw" Small who earned his whiskey by biting off the heads of living snakes and frogs, left their mark here. "Snap Jaw" made it to "Michigan's Boot Hill" after biting off the head of another lumberjack's pet owl. Then there were "Pump Handle Joe" and "Protestant Bob" McGuire and "Stub Foot" O'Donnell, bar room brawlers of the most murderous sort.

If you head straight south of town for a mile or so, you will come to the old cemetery, "Michigan's Boot Hill". Lots of these fellas and many others were buried there. Most of the graves are still there, but only one or two markers have survived the passing years. Many were buried with no records kept at all. You can learn about those days by visiting the local historical museum, open all summer long. They have lots of artifacts and old records. You can find out about "Wiry" Jim Summers, "Frying Pan Mag" and more.

There was another famous lumber man who survived his time in Seney, "Silver Jack" Driscoll. His legend is large, from the Tittabawassee River all the way to the Huron Mountains, and it is in those mountains where he claimed to have found a gold mine. After 1893 "Silver Jack" spent his last days in L'Anse, fighting, drinking, and brawling as always. When he ran out of money, he would head north into the Huron Mountains, a trackless wilderness that is still one of the most remote areas in Michigan. "Silver Jack" would reappear after a couple of weeks, resupplied with gold nuggets, and sometimes silver. He would hang around the saloons until he was broke, then head out again. Concerned citizens tried to track him into the mountains, no doubt concerned that he would twist an ankle or get mauled by a bear and need help, but he would always elude them. Soon he would be back with more nuggets. He never divulged the location of his mine and the secret of its location is now lost, just like "Silver Jack"s" final resting place.

Directions: The village of Seney is at the junction of Route 77 and Route 28. The cemetery and the historical museum are just south of 28.

THE

MINDEN

BOG

IS

THE

LAST

TRUE

RAISED

BOG

IN

MICHIGAN

MINDEN BOG

This is a destination for nature lovers who like it rough. About mid-way up the "thumb" of Michigan, and a bit inland from Lake Huron, is a very unusual area known as the Minden Bog. If you visit in an early morning mist or at dusk when the fireflies emerge, it is easy to imagine the ghosts of lost adventurers wandering across the wind swept heath. This is a giant wetland of around 5,000 acres. At one time the Minden Bog may have covered 30 square miles. It is still so large that it shows up as a dark area, on satellite photographs of Michigan.

The Minden Bog is a raised bog, which gives it a dome shape ,with the top being about 200 feet above Lake Huron. This feature is not very evident when you are there, but that doesn't diminish the experience. About a third of this peat-land is within the Minden State Game Area, and this is also the headlands of the Cass and Black Rivers.

This is a rough hike because the paths are all animal trails. That just adds to the wilderness feeling. There is a wide variety of wild flowers and shrubs. There is ample evidence of a beaver population. After hiking just a short way into the bog, it is easy to lose your sense of direction. When you get far enough in, every direction looks the same. There are no buildings, few trees, and fewer landmarks. It is not recommended that you enter this area alone. There are holes in the ground, ditches, water, and no facilities.

This is an interesting place at any time of day. If you want a bog wilderness to explore, this is the spot. At dawn or dusk it will simply take your breath away. There just isn't any other place like this in the "thumb". There are no facilities of any kind.

Directions: The Minden Bog is southwest of Minden City and west of Palms. From Route 25 between Port Sanilac and Forestville, take the road to Palms. Pass through Palms heading west, and after a mile or so the paved road will curve to the north. Continue west on the gravel road for a couple of miles, and you will reach a dead end. You can park there. A small path leads west to a foot bridge across a canal, and into the bog.

MONARCH BUTTERFLY MIGRATION

Back in the 1950s & 60s, the Michigan Department of Natural Resources, regularly received reports of strange twisting clouds, drifting through the sky, high above Lake Michigan. These reports always came in during the autumn season, usually from folks on color tours, around the Leelanau peninsula. The DNR generally dismissed the reports as having no validity. Perhaps a little too much cherry wine was being consumed. After digital cameras became common, it was discovered that the unusual clouds were real, and that they were actually enormous flocks of Monarch butterflies, on their winter migration route to Mexico. This migration has been repeated for centuries and continues today. There is no need to search for strange clouds, floating above the lake. Instead, there is a place you can visit, where the butterflies pause to rest, before beginning the long journey to the mountains of Mexico.

Every autumn, during the last two weeks of August, and the first two weeks of September, the Monarchs appear at Stonington Point, a beautiful spot that lies between the Big and Little Bays De Noc, in the upper peninsula. Here, they gather in the trees and on the bushes, by the tens of thousands. When the winds are right, they take off in fantastic numbers, forming enormous clouds of butterflies. The migration flight heads south across Lake Michigan, across Green Bay, and on, to their winter home in the mountains of Mexico. A flight that will require about five weeks.

In the summer breeding months, Monarch butterflies have a lifespan of 2 – 6 weeks. However, the generation that makes the flight to Mexico lives longer, long enough to make the flight to Mexico, and is known as the Methuselah generation. That generation lives all winter, and make the return flight to the north. Upon arrival, they resume the normal life cycle of 2 – 6 weeks. When it is time to gather again, for the flight to Mexico, none of the butterflies in the new generation will have made the flight before. How this new generation knows when and where to gather, and the route to Mexico the correct place in Mexico, is one of the enduring mysteries in nature.

Some say that the Monarchs gather on the Garden Peninsula, and a few do, but the real action is at Stonington Point. The specific day the butterflies arrive on the point is unpredictable, but many flocks do land during the last two weeks in August, and the first two weeks in September. If you visit the peninsula during those weeks, and they are not there, just come back every day or so. The point itself is several acres, with a 3 story lighthouse, that is open if you want to climb to the top. There are several picnic areas, interpretive signs, and, if you are there on the right day, thousands of Monarch butterflies.

The Stonington Point peninsula lies between the Big and Little Bays De Noc. Escanaba is directly across the little bay to the west. If you plan to stay in the area for several days, hoping to walk among the butterflies, the Nahma Inn in Nahma, Michigan, has comfortable lodgings and good food.

Directions: Travel west from the Mackinac Bridge on U.S. 2, past Manistique and continue on toward Rapid River. A small sign, with a depiction of a lighthouse, says Stonington Point 17 miles south. Sixteen of those miles are paved, and end at a parking area. The last mile to the point, is a gravel road, through the cedar wetlands. You can drive the last mile, or enjoy the easy walk along the bay.

THE

OCTAGON

BARN

IS

THE

LARGEST

OF

ITS

TYPE

IN

AMERICA

OCTAGON BARN

James Purdy was traveling through Iowa when he saw an octagonal barn for the first time. He talked with local farmers who extolled the virtues of the octagon shape. Not only did it provide more usable storage in the same square footage as a rectangular barn, it made the work space more organized. Mr. Purdy was so impressed that he decided to build one of his own. He needed land for the barn, and began purchasing acres in 1895.

This is easily the most unusual barn anywhere in the region. It is the largest timber frame octagon barn in the country at 102 feet across and 70 feet high. When construction began in 1924, it was known as an air castle because the entire vast interior is open and the roof seems to be suspended above. There is plenty to see when visiting the Octagon Barn. The site has several historic structures including the Purdy House, a one room schoolhouse, sawmill, cide r mill, and a covered bridge. The covered bridge allows visitors access to buildings on both sides of a ditch. The siding used for the bridge is original siding from the barn from before it was restored.

What exists on this site today is the result of a vision, a team effort, generous contributions and many hours of planning, organization, and plain hard work. The vision began in the minds of a few neighbors who did not want to see such an awesome structure and piece of agricultural history be destroyed in the name of 'convenience' or 'progress'.

And so began the Friends of the Thumb Octagon Barn organization - a rescue effort to save the barn from demolition, then restore the barn, then restore the house and surrounding grounds. Fund-raising efforts have grown into annual events known around the state. The vision to preserve has grown into a plan to own and operate an educational/historical/agricultural site for the education, recreation and entertainment of the community and visitors. There is a cool harvest festival here each autumn.

Directions: The Octagon Barn is located in Tuscola County west from Caro, approximately 1 mile east of the Village of Gagetown along Bay City Forestville Road 1 mile north on Richie Road, just south of the Huron County border.

ODDITY AT NEGWEGON

We think of camping and roasted marshmallows when we think of State Parks in Michigan. Most state parks in Michigan are convenient places to take a camper, they provide facilities and showers, and beautiful camp sites in the trees. There are a few that are more rustic, and one, Negwegon State Park, is not only downright wild, it also contains a couple of mysteries worth exploring.

This lakeside nature area is mostly unimproved. You park in a designated area, and then must hike into the park, to one of only four campsites. If not there for camping, you can also hike to the nearby beach on Lake Huron or take the long loop hike through the forest. The first campsite, #1, is more than a quarter mile in. The northernmost campsite, #4, is nearly two miles with a view of the Bird Islands. Each campsite is secluded from the others and each contains only rustic facilities.

There is a gravel parking lot at the entrance. There are vault style comfort facilities and there is an artesian well flowing, so you can fill your canteen.

If you hike toward the sound of Lake Huron, in a short while you will reach a secluded beach, that is as wild as it was before the area was settled. For campers the trail into the park is at the north end of the parking lot. You have to walk as no motorized vehicles are allowed. Campers need to bring everything, there is no store or ranger office. The nearest town is miles away so take everything you need. The path is well maintained but can be wet.

The trail is the easiest way to reach the campsites. After you pass Campsite 3 you will come to a fork in the trail. Stay to the right and you will enter a rather large meadow. If you keep on through the meadow you will reach Campsite 4. The Bird Islands are offshore, and the lights of Alpena are visible in the distance, after dark.

Now, about those mysteries, wander around the meadow for a while and you will discover two separate ruins. One appears to be the foundations of a dwelling. The other is an old, old stone well. The story is told that during the late 1800s, a free black man lived here, all alone. He lived in his cabin, hunting, trapping, and fishing. Every spring he would travel to Black River to trade pelts for luxuries, like sugar and coffee. One spring, he didn't show up. The traders at Black River noticed his absence, he was the only black resident of Alcona County. They decided to go check up on the reclusive trapper. Upon arrival, everything seemed to be in order. The well contained water. The cabin was in good repair and everything inside was as it should be. There was plenty of food, the traps, tools, and weapons were there. In the out building, the pelts and furs were properly stored, and baled for transport. The only thing missing was the black man. He was never found or heard from again. He had simply disappeared without a trace. Hike into this wilderness during the winter, and you will wonder how anyone could survive in this remote location, 100 years ago, all alone.

Then there are the old stone walls, cairns, and ruins. To find them, you take the left branch of the fork in the trail, just before the meadow. Hike another hundred yards and you arrive at a small stream that crosses the path. Turn to the left and follow the stream into the trees and eventually into a swampy area. In early spring or after the first hard frost in the fall, the undergrowth will be sparse. Searching carefully one can find the old stone construction. It consists of long stone walls with right angles. There are rooms and enclosures defined by walls that are about three feet high. There are also very unusual round structures that look like nothing I have seen. They were reported as cairns by trappers and others. The round structures are 6 – 10 feet across and 4 feet high in some cases, and there are a lot of them. This site is easily the size of two football fields. No one knows when it was constructed, who did it, or what purpose it served. To protect this site, I don't give exact directions. The local historical society can help with that.

Another unusual feature near here is underwater. At one time there was a land bridge from near Alpena, across Lake Huron to Canada, referred to as the Alpena-Amberly Ridge. On this land bridge, now way under water, man made constructions have been discovered. Specifically, caribou channeling structures used to force migrating caribou into killing zones. Interestingly, the photos of these structures shows them to be almost identical to ones in use in the far north that are still accessible. There are also stone cairns visible. All of this has been preserved by the pure still waters of Lake Huron. These structures are very old. It is estimated that when they were in use, the glacier that was receding was only 100 miles north and was still a mile high. That would have been a very harsh hunting environment. It is not known who built these structures either.

Directions: Negwegon State Park is located on the shores of Lake Huron a few miles north of Black River. The park is reached by land after driving along a very rough sand trail for several miles. It is actually easier to get there on the water by canoe or kayak.

THE

NEWBERRY

STONES

ARE

ON

DISPLAY

INSIDE

THE

FORT

DE

BUADE

MUSEUM

ODDITY AT ST. IGNACE

In 1896, a tremendous wind storm, swept across the upper peninsula. Buildings were damaged, and hundreds of century old trees, were uprooted. One of the trees the storm blew over, was on the farm of John McGuer, north of Newberry. According to the Soo Evening News, several mysterious objects were stuck in the root system, of an enormous old hemlock, felled by that storm. The items included 3 statues and a large stone tablet. The tablet was engraved with strange inscriptions.

The largest statue was nearly life size, and seemed to depict a man, sitting on a sort of pedestal. The second, appeared to be a woman, and is a bit smaller. The third and smallest statue, seems to be the image of a child. All three are of sandstone, and had the appearance of great age. The tablet, found nearby, was about 18" by 25". One side, was covered with 140 inscriptions, engraved in rows. Each row, was made up of squares, about 1 ½ inches in size.

For many weeks after the discovery, these odd artifacts were on display, in a store in Newberry. While speculation ran wild, no one then or now, has come up with an answer to the question of origin. Nor has there been a consensus, on a coherent translation, of the tablet inscriptions. Photos were submitted to universities, scholars, and experts, and were pretty much poo – pooed, although excellent photos were taken by the Smithsonian, and were published in Issue 71, of Ancient American.

Eventually, the furor died down, and the four pieces were stored away in the McGruer barn, and suffered a lot of damage through the years. Sometime around 1929, the remnants were gathered up, and moved to a small museum, at Fort Algonquin, where they were stored away under the stairs, and were pretty much forgotten, except by the occasional searcher.

Many stories, about mysterious artifacts, end with the objects being lost somehow, but not in this case. Excellent photographs, and original newspaper articles, exist. Even better, the parts of the statues, and a portion of the tablet, have been preserved. The years have been hard on these artifacts, but they are now protected, and are on display, at the Fort De Buade Museum in downtown St. Ignace. Photos, reprints and attempted translations of the tablet, await anyone who is curious. One translation of the Newberry Stone Tablet, is by Barry Fell. His position was, that the tablet depicts a magic quadrangle, and should be read both vertically and horizontally, in alternate directions. He further purported, that these magical charms, were probably copies of something from the eastern Mediterranean. The text is said to be ancient Hittite-Minoan. The translation is a bit cryptic, as one would expect, and is on display at the museum.

Research continues to determine the origin of the objects and translation of the tablet. The museum is operated by the Michilimackinac Historical Society, and, in addition to the Newberry Tablet, has over 6,000 square feet of exhibits. The museum is at 334 N. State Street in St. Ignace and is open May 30 – October 1.

ALPENA

IS

THE

ONLY

PLACE

THIS

KIND

OF

DISC

HAS

DISCOVERED

ODDITY AT THUNDER BAY

Unusual artifacts have been dug up all over the Great Lakes Region, and North America, for that matter. Huge skulls, slabs with strange inscriptions, and medieval weapons to name a few. The oddity, or oddities, discovered near Alpena are completely unique. Nothing like them has been discovered anywhere else. The sheer number alone sets this discovery apart.

Apparently, near the mouth of the Thunder Bay River, there was a place dedicated to the manufacture of unique discs. These discs were fashioned from shale taken from a local source. The time of this activity has been estimated to be between 1250 A.D. - 1400 A.D. In that time several hundred discs were created.

The main site was known as the Hampsher site. Here hundreds of the discs were discovered in varying stages of completion. The discs are small, only an inch or two in diameter. They were roughed out and then smoothed. Some of the discs have inscriptions and some have small hole drilled through as though these would be worn as a necklace. Among the symbols engraved on the discs are "Ne-gig" the otter, "Moz" the moose, "Amik" the beaver, a tree, and a star form. In addition to these, two very special engravings occur. One is the Thunderbird - "Ah-ne-mi-ke" and the other is the Water Tiger - "Me-she-pe-shiw" depicted with a long tail, horns, and clawed feet.

Native American traditions held that the Thunderbird caused the thunder and lightning storms. The Water Tiger lived beneath the waters of Thunder Bay and cause the violent storms that endangered travelers on the lake. In fact, the Water Tiger was said to inhabit all five of the Great Lakes. Interestingly, the discs with the Thunderbird and Water Tiger do not have holes drilled in them. It has been speculated that these special symbols would have been kept in an individuals medicine bag, rather than being worn around the neck as an amulet. Only some of the recovered discs were engraved. Among the engravings used, the Medicine Tree occurs the most often. Oddly, some discs that have a hole drilled in them have no engraving or inscription.

The discovery of these discs revealed several mysteries. This is the only place in Michigan where amulets of this type have been discovered. In fact, this is the only place in North America. The period of manufacture was relatively short, and was limited to this small geographic area. Yet, similar symbols have been found in petroglyphs on the Canadian Shield near Petersborough, Canada. Some have suggested that the symbols on some of the discs are similar to those found in the Mide-Wi-Win birch bark scrolls. The original meanings and purposes of the discs remain unknown.

The discovery of this, and three other sites, is attributed to Robert E. Haltiner and his father Gerald. The 4 sites have been designated, Hampsher, Anderson, Van Lare Hall, and Hooley Creek. The Hampsher site proved to be the most productive.

The Hooley Creek site has been destroyed due to mining and quarry activity. The Van Lare Hall site, on the campus of Alpena College, is gone due to development.

The discs have been given the name, Naub-cow-zo-win. This is a term from the Algonquian people that translates roughly as 'charms of personal significance'. These enigmatic discs have been preserved. They are on display at the Jesse Besser Museum in Alpena, Michigan. They are part of the excellent primitive man exhibit.

PESTILENCE HOUSE

Directly across from the Dark Sky entrance, is the Mackinaw Historical Society Heritage Village. The complex consists of a variety of historic structures from about 1880 through 1917. This was a period of dramatic changes in transportation, communication, housing, health care, and nearly every other aspect of life. The last existing Pest House in Michigan is part of the village. A Pestilence House is a quarantine facility that was found in nearly every Michigan community around 1900. This example was built in the 1890s, and was rediscovered in 2004. It had been used as a machine shop, but had been abandoned.

Pest Houses could be found in almost every small Michigan town. In those years, smallpox was a real danger, along with diptheria and cholera. This was an era when germs and viruses were poorly understood. The local doctor might also be the barber and bleeding was still used as a treatment. Quarantine was the most used procedure to stop the spread of contagious diseases. No one yet realized how important something as basic as clean hands was. Hand washing would have been a complex undertaking. There was no running water. It had to be hauled to the Pest House in buckets. In winter, the water had to be warmed, on a wood burning stove. Patients of all ages and genders were housed in the same building. The different areas may have been separated by nothing more than cloth curtains. Infected persons remained inside until they were better. One in three individuals didn't survive.

Advances in medical treatment made Pestilence Houses obsolete. Pest Houses that weren't re-purposed deteriorated and fell apart, or were dismantled and destroyed. This is the only intact Michigan example I have found. It has been faithfully restored. The village covers about 140 acres with lots of unique and one-of-a-kind buildings. One example is the the bone room, a small kiosk with hands on displays that will fascinate kids of all ages.

Directions: The Mackinaw Historical Society Heritage Village is located about two miles west of downtown Mackinaw City in northwest lower

Michigan. From downtown Mackinaw City, head west on Central Avenue, the main street through the downtown. The entrance to the village is just east of Headlands Road.

THE

SANILAC

PETROGLYPHS

ARE

THE

ONLY

SUCH

CARVINGS

IN

MICHIGAN

SANILAC PETROGLYPHS

There are a number of ways to interpret the meaning of the prehistoric carvings, in the forest in Sanilac County. There are even conflicting stories about how they were rediscovered. Here is one story of that discovery. In 1871, farmers were using fires to clear their land. Those fires got out of control, destroying 2 million acres of forest and killing 200 people. In 1881, another fire swept across the thumb. This fire burned a million acres in one day and killed 282 people. The fires and heat were so intense that railroad rails were twisted and entire towns were obliterated. After the fire, strong west winds blew through, the topsoil was swept away, revealing the long hidden carvings. It is interesting to note that, there is no mention of these carvings in any writings or oral histories, prior to the 1870s firestorms.

There are hundreds of images carved into a large sandstone outcropping. Some of the more unusual images, like the 6 finger hand, and the archer with the conical hat, still offer puzzles to be solved. There are carvings that are readily understood, like the coyote, rabbit, and bird tracks. There are spirals similar to those found in carvings all over the world. Then there are the carvings that seem to be representations of fantastic animals or even, as some say, unusual letters and scripts. The trail of coyote tracks that cross the sandstone are part of the carvings and run almost perfectly south to north.

Some of the petroglyphs are difficult to interpret. There are unidentified animal, and symbolic shapes. There are several interpretations of the meaning and origins of the carvings. One interpretation of the archer with the conical hat is that he represents a "holy man". The arrow represents knowledge and truth. When it is launched by the bow, it sends these virtues into the future, through the education of the young. The conical hat represents the two sides of human nature, the conscious and the spiritual. One side of the hat represents hopes and aspirations. The other side represents faith and prayers. The conical shape of the hat symbolizes both being sent upward, to the heavens. Again, this is just one of the many interpretations of this particular glyph.

The sandstone outcropping is protected by a fence and a roof. During the summer season volunteers are on hand to allow visitors to get up close to the carvings. They also offer an entertaining and educational program describing the carvings. This program is the best way to get accurate information about the interpretations of the petroglyphs.

There is an excellent walking trail at this site. The main trail is one loop of about a mile. It winds through the forest and crosses the Cass River, via small suspension bridges, in two places. The trail is narrow in places, and can be rough, due to tree roots growing near the surface. The topography is quite varied. The forest and undergrowth are very dense where the trail crosses the river or passes near wetlands. In a couple of places, beaver activity has dammed the river forming small ponds. Then there are the huge rock formations. Giant slabs of rock are visible along the way. Many of these were underwater at one time, back when the Cass River was nearly a mile wide. Another unique feature of this trail is the towering White Pine growing just off the trail. This tree is estimated to be over 125 years old. It probably sprouted right after the the last of the great firestorms in 1881. Those firestorms, and the winds that followed, helped expose the petroglyphs.

Directions: From Highway 25 on the Lake Huron shore, take Bay City-Forestville Rd. west to Germania Rd. Go south about 1/2 mile and you will reach the park where these remarkable carvings are located.

SHRINE OF THE PINES

The Shrine of the Pines is known as a "rustic furniture museum". It is certainly that, but there is more to the story. The museum sits in a small stand of pines on the famous Pere' Marquette River. That setting is perfect for this historic display of craftsmanship from another era. The contents of this Michigan treasure are the life work of Raymond W. Overholzer. Inside the log cabin, that serves as the museum, are over 200 pieces of his incredible rustic work.

This is the largest collection of rustic pine furniture in the world. The workmanship of this artisan is so fine, that it is hard to think of these pieces as "rustic furniture". It is also hard to believe, that everything here is the work of one man. Not only that, it was done without power tools. Mr. Overholzer collected and processed every piece of wood necessary for his masterpieces. He developed his own finishes and did all of the inlay work by hand. These are more than just a table, beds, rocking chair, and other furniture. Many pieces hold some secret hiding place, that may not be obvious at first glance.

The large dining table was crafted from one white pine stump. It is more than 7 feet across and weighs in excess of 700 pounds. The finish on it, like most of the work here, is drop dead gorgeous. The tour guide will probably show you some of the hidden compartments that are artistically concealed in the construction. The rocking chair is made mostly of roots. It too, is special. While it may look like other "rustic" rockers you have seen, this one is so well balanced, that one push will set it to rocking, and it will keep rocking, for more than 50 repetitions. The stunning fireplace is made of 70 tons of stone. There is a wooden gun rack with 39 wooden ball bearings and much more. Even the windows and window frames are works of art. The tour is fun and informative. The museum is open during the tourism season.

Outside are some tranquil trails running through the white pine forest. These woodlands paths are wheelchair accessible. The forest and the river attract wildlife and a wide variety of birds. You can even watch the trout in the river, from the museum observation deck.

Directions: Located just south of downtown Baldwin, Michigan on route M-37. Baldwin is about one hour north of Grand Rapids.

THERE

ARE

ONLY

FIVE

MINI

COOPER

SPEEDER

CARS

IN

THE

WORLD

SPEEDER CARS

Railroads were vital to the development of Michigan. The rail companies followed the lumber industry north creating a web of railroads connecting communities, shipping ports, and remote stands of timber. As the railroads grew, so did the need for maintenance. The hand-powered rail handcar was the first vehicle developed to travel the rails on inspection runs. Then, sometime in the 1890s, the U.S. Daimler Motor Company, created a gasoline powered inspection car. It could only go 15 mph, but that was faster than the old handcar. That was the beginning of what would become Speeder Cars. Eventually, Speeders could get up to around 35 mph, and were used for inspection and maintenance all over the world. In the 1990s, Speeders went out of use. They were replaced by pick up trucks fitted with small rail wheels that could be lowered onto railroad tracks. Speeders were replaced, but they are not gone.

Speeder Car enthusiasts have organized to preserve and restore the cars. Speeders look like boxy little vehicles sitting on small rail car wheels. They are sometimes open, sometimes closed, and about the size of the old pump handcars. They are so cool that there is a Speeder Car Excursion through Northern Michigan every year. The excursion, usually in June, starts in Cadillac, goes to Petoskey and comes back to Cadillac via Kalkaska. They make several stops along the way so folks can come out, and check them out.

When the Speeder Cars pause in a town, kids of all ages gather to climb aboard. During the excursion, you can be at a planned stop. Soon, here they come, red, green, yellow, in all kinds of configurations and colors. In the 2016 excursion, there was a Speeder Car with a Mini Cooper as the cab, mounted on a speeder chassis. It is one of only 5, Mini Cooper Speeders, in the world. There are Speeder Cars from across the United States and Canada that join the event.

Other terms for speeders included railway motor car, putt-putt, track-maintenance car, crew car, jigger, trike, quad, trolley, and inspection car.

STORY IN THE STONES

As we hurry along our way we often overlook the structures that hold our history and tell our stories. Examples of unusual or historic architecture can be found all over Michigan. The Burner in Nahma, the Bottle House in Kaleva, and the Octagon Barn near Gagetown, are good examples. Another building with stories hidden in its architecture, is the Village Hall in Bellevue, Michigan.

At the flashing light in downtown Bellevue, the Village Hall sits on the northwest corner. You can't miss it. It is a two story structure that is unique for the exterior stonework. There is plenty of parking downtown, so it is convenient to walk around this building, and study the handiwork of the artisan who carved these stones. This is all rock faced field stone and is the work of Charles H. Secore. As you take in the details you will realize that these were not simply cut and mortared in. There are unusual patterns here. Stones were cut into circles, diamonds, and even a large arrowhead. The arrowhead on the south wall is about three feet long. To fit these unusual shapes into the walls required skills not readily found today. The building was completed in the early 1900s and was originally a bank.

It turns out that these stones tell a bit of the history of the area. The large circular stones, are said to represent the medicine wheels of the Ojibway and Chippewa tribes, who inhabited the area. The diamond is a symbol, used to represent the four directions, by the Ojibway. The tall vertical arrow head, is a Chippewa reference, since they were known for making arrowheads. There are more intricately carved stones including one in the shape of a heart. The entire exterior is a work of art that we would have difficulty producing today. The interior of this building has been preserved. The mosaic tile floor is intact, the elaborate woodwork is polished and the original bank vault is still there and in use for storing files.

If you decide to check out the Story In The Stones, here are a few things to see, so you can make a day of it. During a construction project on a nearby farm, the bones of a huge mastodon were discovered. The Village is planning an interactive museum for the discovery. In the library building, you can find the Historical Museum. About two blocks east is the old historic mill. It has been restored and is producing electricity from the river water flowing through turbines in the basement. On the way out of town west, is the Bellevue Drive In, famous for the incredible onion rings they make there. Across the street from the drive in is a restored one room schoolhouse. Turn south at that road and come to the old Dyer Limestone Kiln. Across the road is the entrance to the Kheene Environmental Area that is the site of the original limestone quarry. Limestone from this quarry was prepared in the kiln, and was used in the construction of the state capitol building in Lansing. It is cool to find all of this in a village of just 1,400.

Directions: Downtown Bellevue is mid-way between Lansing and Battle Creek. From Route 66 north of Battle Creek take M-78 east about 7 miles. From I-69 south of Charlotte take either Bellevue exit.

COLANTHA

WAS

THE

ONLY

RESIDENT

BURIED

ON

THE

GROUNDS

OF

THE

MICHIGAN

ASYLUM

TOMBSTONES

Cemeteries can be found in towns large and small, and all along the back roads. There is even a tiny triangle shaped cemetery north of Centreville. Each of the three sides is defined by a road, so the cemetery is actually defined by crossroads. Then there are the unusual or historic tombstones, that can be found across the state. One example is the story of the "glowing tombstones" in Evart, elsewhere in this book. Here are a few other notable tombstones.

1. During the war between the states, Confederate cavalry commander JEB Stuart was well known for his skill and daring, as well as, his flamboyant style of dress. On May 11, 1864 he was conducting operations near the Yellow Tavern north of Richmond, Virginia. During the battle, the 5th Michigan was retreating. Among them was forty-five year old John A. Huff. Huff, who had served as a sharpshooter for two years, noticed a Confederate officer on horseback. The man had a pistol and was smartly turned out in a silk-lined cape, a black plume in his hat, and a bright yellow sash. Huff paused, aimed his pistol carefully and fired at the figure on horseback from about 30 feet away, then rejoined the retreat. This unlikely encounter was the end of JEB Stuart. He was struck by that one bullet and the wound proved fatal. John Huff is buried in Armada, Michigan. His grave has only a simple marker.

2. Joseph Coveney, a prominent land owner, was one of the wealthiest men in the Buchanan area back in the 1800s. He was well known for holding controversial opinions and for being an atheist. He wanted a special monument for his burial plot but was unable to find a local stonecutter willing to carve the engravings he wanted. Mr. Coveney went about having his monument carved in England. When it arrived here in Michigan, he went ahead and had it installed in the Oak Ridge Cemetery. The furor erupted immediately. Near the top of the monument, on the four sides, appeared the phrases: "Free Religion," "Free Press," "Free Speech" and "Free Thought". In other places on the monument were other freethinker statements like, "All Christian denominations preach damnation," "The more priests the more poverty," "The more religion the more lying," "The more saints the more hypocrites" and "Nature is the true God, Science is the true religion." Other statements are even more controversial. The horror and outrage in the community was nearly universal, but there was nothing that could be done. Mr. Coveney was to enjoy the controversy he caused for another 20 years before he passed. The monument is still there, though the inscriptions are badly deteriorated.

3. Nisula is a tiny settlement in the western upper peninsula. There isn't much there now, and most folks just roll through, hardly slowing down. On the south side of the road, Route 38, sits an old style white church. The church stands among the gravestones, in a cemetery, that has been there for more than a century. On the west side of the the church is a most unusual tombstone. It stands out from all the others. It is about three feet tall, is shaped like a pyramid, and is deep black in color with some sparkles. Legend has it, that this tombstone was a meteor, that fell on a local farm in the 1800s. The farmer recovered the meteor and brought it home. It is told that his wife loved the appearance of the stone and got her family to promise to have it engraved as her grave marker.

4. Sometimes a rise to world fame has very humble beginnings; and so it was for Colantha Walker. She lived her entire life as a resident of the Northern Michigan Asylum.

The Northern Michigan Asylum opened in 1885. It eventually grew into a giant complex on the outskirts of Traverse City, Michigan. In fact, at one point, the population of the hospital complex, 3,500, was greater than the population of the city. The Asylum was self-sufficient with its own farms, gardens, fire department, and power plant. It had its own orchards of peaches, apples, and cherries, its own vineyards and vegetable gardens, field crops, and a wide variety of livestock, including a herd of cows. The most famous of these, actually the most famous inhabitant of the asylum period, was Colantha Walker, a grand champion milk cow.

In her long and storied career - from 1916 to 1932 - she produced 200,114 pounds of milk and 7,525 pounds of butterfat. In her best year, 1926, her annual production was a world record 22,918 pounds of milk. The official state average was 3,918 pounds. When Colantha went to her reward in 1932, the staff and patients of the asylum, held a banquet in her honor, and erected a huge granite tombstone over her grave.

The Asylum closed in 1989, but the 500 acre property is being revitalized. The old asylum buildings are creamy brick and are architecturally spectacular. The complex is being transformed into an entire town with unique shops, galleries, restaurants, apartments and condominiums. Even if the tomb were not there, it is worth a visit just to see the gigantic structure that was once the asylum.

The Tomb of the Cow is tucked away on the south edge of the property near the old original barns. At a curve in the road just south of two champion Black Willows, the engraved stone sits between two trees. She is the only resident of the asylum to be buried on the grounds. Colantha's accomplishments are commemorated by a Dairy Festival on the grounds each year.

THE

MODEL

CITY

WAS

KNOWN

AS

THE

MECHANICAL

WONDER

OF

THE

AGES

TREASURE IN CAPAC

The original Kempf Model City was constructed in the early 1900s by Fred S. Kempf. He completed the work between the ages of 16 and 21. He made every single part, by hand, from scrap materials. The Model City was hailed as one of the most remarkable constructions of the time, and was shown at events all over America. Then during a terrible train crash, the model city was destroyed. Fred Kempf and his wife lost their lives in that same train wreck in 1915.

Bruce and Irving Kempf began construction on a new model city that eventually was hailed as the "Mechanical Wonder of the Age". The Model City is a mechanical city, built to the scale of 1/8 inch to the foot. It is 40 feet in length by 4 feet wide. The entire Model City is operated by a ½ horsepower motor, found in the mountain, at the end of the city. The city was fully operational and depicts a typical American city in the 1920s. The city is fully populated with hand-carved people and has all the necessities of life. Cars that travel along the streets are serviced by a corner gasoline station. When they wear out, there is even a junkyard filled with tires and rusted iron. The new mechanical wonder had more than 17,000 moving parts.

For 19 years the city was displayed from coast to coast and throughout Canada: The Century of Progress, Chicago: Atlantic City's Steel Pier: Great Lakes Exposition, Cleveland: and Lakeside Park, Denver, Canadian National Exhibition and all the major State Fairs in the United States. During the Christmas seasons it was displayed in major department stores across the United States, and many large movie lobbies, from New York City to San Francisco. The Model City went into storage at the onset of WW II and was moved to Grand Blanc, Michigan. In 1988, the Capac Historical Museum purchased the mechanical wonder city.

Inside the Capac Historical Museum the "Mechanical Wonder of the Ages" is on display. It is being refurbished. The Model City is remarkable for its size and detail. When fully functioning, it looks like an actual living city. Lights inside most of the structures reveal that life in "Model City" is not restricted to the streets. A man rocks comfortably in a chair inside the Maxwell Coffee House, and a new fire engine is poised inside the doors of the fire station. Blue lights flash on and off at the welding factory, indicating a night shift at work. A general store on the main drag displays bananas and other fresh fruit. All the more remarkable is the fact that the whole thing runs on small sewing machine motors and belts, no transistors and no computer chips.

The train wreck that destroyed the original mechanical wonder was described as "horrific" and the cars were quickly engulfed in flames. One of the last acts of the lives of Fred and Blanche Kempf was to literally, throw their infant daughter out the window of the train. That act saved her life. In 1988, Bruce and Irving's niece, Hazel Kempf Mack, the little girl whose life was saved the day of the train crash that killed her parents, located the Model City in Grand Blanc. Events were set in motion that returned the city to its home in Capac. The history, the photos and the "Mechanical Wonder of the Ages" are housed in Capac at the museum.

Directions: Capac is west of Port Huron.

THE

ANIMATED

DOLLS

WERE

ONCE

PART

OF

A

DEPARTMENT

STORE

DISPLAY

TREASURE IN HART

Step Into The Past - The downtown Hart Historic District contains the most historical buildings and collections in Oceana County. The district is located on the edge of Chippewa Creek. This was an old business section on the site of the Centennial Northern Market Chesapeake Ohio Railroad deadhead. Several historical collections are on display.

A one of a kind treasure is the exhibit, of Animated Dolls, guaranteed to amaze and delight boys and girls of all ages. The displays depict scenes from daily life from the pioneer era, from playing a piano, to churning butter, to feeding the baby. When you enter the doll area of the museum it all seems fairly normal, just old dolls and puppets on display. Then they turn on the power and the dolls and puppets all around you spring into action. All of it is mechanical, computer animation hadn't been invented yet.

The scenes and animation are so cool that smiles breakout and everyone begins to clap. There is a lumber jack scene, an entire choir, a washer woman laboring, sisters in bunk beds where the girl in the upper is teasing the girl in the lower with a feather, cowboys playing banjos. These fantastic dolls were originally used in displays at the, now closed, Powers Department Store in Hart. There just isn't another display like this anywhere in Michigan.

In a separate building is another remarkable collection. On display is one of the largest collections of Native American tools and arrow tips anywhere in Michigan. The display of carved effigies alone is worth the trip.

Directions: The Hart Historic District in Hart, Michigan is at the corner of Washington and Union Streets, four blocks east the main street in downtown.

TREASURE IN MECOSTA

Tucked away in central Michigan, is the tiny settlement of Mecosta. People who take the road through Mecosta are usually on their way somewhere else, and are often in a hurry, so they drive right by the treasure.

Inside an old building on the main street that, at first glance, appears to be shut down, is a collection of more than 75,000 books. This is the Mecosta Book Gallery. There are stacks of books in several rooms. Many of the titles are rare, or out of print, or both. Another unique feature of this treasure trove, is that the proprietors don't automatically make them available on the web.

When you enter, you are instantly in the stacks. Narrow aisles run throughout the store. The books are stacked to the high ceiling in every direction. For a book lover with some spare time, this is a paradise. The service here is casual, but excellent. I was once searching for an out-of-print book about Michigan and couldn't locate it anywhere in the state. I chanced to be on my way, somewhere else, and detoured to Mecosta. It took less than five minutes for the man in charge to walk me to the exact spot where the treasure I sought was waiting.

Across the street is the other bookstore run by these folks. I will leave that for you to discover on your own. The shops are open at odd hours throughout the year, but Thursday through Saturday are good bets. Check the Mecosta Book Gallery hours of operation at www.iswara.com.

Directions: Mecosta, Michigan, is on Route 20 just east of Route 66. Mecosta is roughly midway between Mt. Pleasant and Big Rapids.

TREASURE IN MANTON

Manton is a pretty little town up in Wexford County just a few miles east of Mesick. Mesick is home to that world-famous Morel Mushroom Festival. Sportsmen and nature lovers may know of Manton, because the area abounds with trails, parks, lakes and designated trout streams. The section of the Manistee River that flows just north is incredibly beautiful. That is where you can find the Horseshoe Bend. Beautiful as all this is, there is another treasure in town, in fact, a couple of them.

The National Award Winning Veterans Museum was constructed and dedicated in 2002. The museum was entirely achieved by donations of material and labor. The Veteran's Memorial Museum Project was recognized as #1 in the nation by the Veteran's of Foreign Wars. Exhibits feature uniform displays, a military jeep, Japanese swords, a variety of weapons, Civil War items, and over 300 pictures of military personnel, from the Civil War to Vietnam to Desert Storm. The most remarkable treasure you will find here is a trunk, used by a soldier who served under

General George Washington, during the revolutionary war. The Museum is owned by the City of Manton and the Museum Board. It is run and managed by volunteers.

The Manton Pathway and Garden is a 1-1/2 mile nature walk. You will see everything from birds to small animals. There are bridges to cross and benches staggered along the trails. The Manton Pathway and Gardens are open year round Monday - Sunday 8:00 a.m. to 8:00 p.m., and are located ¼ mile north of the US-131 and M-42 intersection, then west on Cedar St. next to the Dairy Bar.

Directions: Manton is located at the crossroads of M-42 & Old U.S. 131.

TREASURE IN SALINE

The Bixby Marionettes are almost unknown to the youth of today. At one time, these remarkable hand-carved puppets, entertained children and adults with shows like Alladin, The Wizard of Oz, The Magic Bean Stalk, and others. Meredith Bixby and his wife, Thyra, began carving the jointed bodies of the puppets at home. They produced the costumes, staging, lighting, scripts, and scenery.

The Meredith Marionettes Touring Company staged shows all across the country in schools, theaters, and community centers. For decades before the advent of the digital age, children waited eagerly for the next show, where animals talked, peasant huts could walk, and good always overcame evil. Every summer the Bixby crew would prepare a new show and open the season by staging it at their studio in Saline. The local kids were the first ones to see the show, that would be seen in person, by a quarter of a million other kids each year.

In 1997 Meredith Bixby made the City of Saline trustee of his collection of marionettes, photos, original art and an extensive collection of other memorabilia. The collection is on display at the District Library on Maple Rd. in Saline, Michigan. Unfortunately, available space is limited so the collection is shown in small parts on a rotating basis. Even so, when you see just a couple of these puppets, you can almost hear the sounds of the wicked magician, as he begins to weave his evil plot.

Directions: Saline is on Route 12, the Great Sauk Trail, just south of Ann Arbor in southeast Michigan. The District Library is on Maple Road near downtown.

TWO GHOST TOWNS

Two Michigan ghost towns separated, by a couple of hundred miles, share a common thread in the history of the Michigan lumber industry. Shaytown was a community west of Lansing, with a working sawmill. Haring grew up north of Cadillac, as the lumbermen pushed north, harvesting the vast forests that had stood for hundreds of years. The great forests are gone, and little is left of either town. The common denominator was one man, Ephraim Shay.

In the early 1870s, Ephraim Shay left his sawmill and Eaton County, and moved to Haring. At this same time, the lumber industry was in deep trouble. The easy flat lands to the south were lumbered out, and key markets were now further away. Most work was still done by men and horses. Some train locomotives were in use, but in rough country, they were unable to negotiate steep grades and icy conditions. By 1873, the cost of moving logs from stump to sawmill had risen to 75% of production cost, and demand was dropping off. Enormous forests still lay to the north, but the lumbermen were going broke.

Ephraim Shay was a mechanical genius, with many innovations to his credit. His Shay Locomotive revolutionized the lumber industry in Michigan, and impacted other industries in rough country, all over the world. The innovation was a departure from the usual approach of trying to build them bigger and faster. The Shay Locomotive employed an ingenious limber drive-shaft. Another innovation was delivering drive power to all wheels increasing traction. The result was a small workhorse, that could turn like a pony, and pull like a mechanical mule. The engine could produce power and traction, to easily handle slippery rails, steep gullies, and sharp turns.

Once the engine was in production, new areas were opened and production costs plummeted. The lumber boom was on again, and was moving north rapidly. In fact, this one innovation improved efficiency so much, that the lumber era was probably shortened by a few decades. There are quite a few of these remarkable locomotives in use around the world, often in the roughest conditions. Six Shay Henderson-style Shays, were built by the Michigan Iron Works in

Cadillac, Michigan. There is one on display in the city park in Cadillac.

A Bit Of History: Almost everyone is familiar with the novel The Wizard Of Oz. The Wonderful Wizard of Oz has long been a favorite story and a number of films have also told the tale. What most people don't know is that The Wonderful Wizard of Oz was only the first in a series of L. Frank Baum's Original "Oz" Series. Titles included, The Wonderful Wizard of Oz, The Marvelous Land of Oz, Ozma of Oz, Dorothy and the Wizard in Oz... and more. The Wexford County Museum in Cadillac has an entire set of the Wizard of Oz books.

Directions: The towns of Haring and Shaytown are gone. Cadillac is on Highway 131 just 100 miles north of Grand Rapids.

THE

TOWERS

WERE

A

POPULAR

DAY

TRIP

DESTINATION

IN

THE

IRISH

HILLS

TWO TOWERS

Travelers heading west from Detroit, or east from Chicago, still enjoy the "Great Sauk Trail", U.S. 12, and the beautiful scenery of the Irish Hills. East of Route 50, on U.S. 12, stand two nearly identical towers, side by side. In 2016, renovations and repairs were underway, to save the towers from demolition. The towers have a unique place, in the history of Michigan tourism, and the Irish Hills.

In the early 1900s, the Irish Hills were a local secret, but Michigan tourism was about to change that. At that time, Cambridge Junction, was about as far as you could get on a day trip, out of Detroit, and still make it back home before dark. Getting back early was important. The roads were sketchy, cars had no headlights, and the area was still a wilderness in some ways.

Edward Kelly owned land along the road, and the Michigan Observation Company wanted to buy a bit of it, with the intention of building a viewing tower. Mr. Kelly declined, but his neighbor, Edward Brighton, agreed, and a 50-foot high tower was built on a high spot, and opened in October of 1924. Just in time for folks to travel out, pay five cents, climb to the top, and gaze out at the spectacular fall colors and brilliant blue lakes, scattered through the hills.

The new tower was just six feet from the property line, and Mr. Kelly was miffed. The observation tower obscured the view from his house. To get even, he built a nearly identical tower, just 12 feet from the original. What's more, he made his tower taller than the original, and the feud was on. The Michigan Observation Company raised their observation platform, so it was equal in height to Kelly's "Spite Tower". Further, they let Mr. Kelly know, that if this didn't put an end to the "feud", they would tear their tower down, and build an enormous steel structure, that would dwarf Kelly's. That did it, and for several years, the competition was in finding unusual ways to attract visitors, even to the point of bringing in alligators and monkeys.

The two towers were a very successful attraction, for more than five decades. At one time, as many as 50 buses per day were bringing tourists, to enjoy the view. The site was open 24 hours per day, and offered, in addition to the zoo, a campground, carnival rides, a dance hall, three gas stations, and a miniature golf course. Lodging was available nearby, and three restaurants served travelers. The advent of the automobile brought more visitors, but also spelled doom for the towers. People could travel further, faster and cheaper, and headed for more impressive destinations. By the mid-1960's more than 2 million people had visited the towers. As time passed, various problems plagued a series of owners, and by the mid-1980's the towers shut down.

The renovation work continues, slowly. Perhaps, one day, the towers will once again welcome visitors to the Irish Hills.

Make A Day Of It: McCourtie Park is to the west at Somerset Center. The park is perfect for a break or a picnic. Stroll along the stream that meanders through the park and admire the 17 bridges. They are all the work of one artist and, they are made of concrete.

Hidden Lake Gardens, a few miles south on Route 223, offers acres of gardens, several walking trails, and unique indoor gardens.

Walker Tavern was a welcome break in the brutal five-day stagecoach ride from Detroit to Chicago. Today, Sylvester Walker's stagecoach stop is a museum open seasonally.

Downtown Saline and downtown Adrian offer excellent places to eat. SASS in Adrian is one of the best shopping destinations in the entire region.

WRECK OF THE ELLENWOOD

On an October night in 1901, the schooner Ella Ellenwood ran aground on Fox Point near the Milwaukee, Wisconsin harbor. Heavily loaded with more than 150 tons of lumber products, the vessel had departed White Lake, on the Michigan side, on schedule. Now, within sight of the safety of the harbor, she was in serious trouble.

Lake Michigan had produced one of her fall storms and, in a few short hours, the schooner Ellenwood was pounded into fragments. The crew was rescued, but the cargo was lost, and the ship itself was completely destroyed. By morning there was nothing left to salvage.

The story has a strange twist. The following year a ships nameplate "ELLENWOOD" washed up on the shore of White Lake, where the disastrous voyage had begun. Somehow the nameplate had drifted across Lake Michigan, and made it into its' home port of White Lake. That nameplate is on display at City Hall in Montague, Michigan.

The Montague City Hall is on the north edge of downtown. They operate a small museum in the basement. That is where the nameplate is displayed along with a complete history of the Ellenwood. When you first arrive in town you will see a gigantic weather vane. It is the largest weather vane in the world. The ship atop the main pole depicts the schooner Ellenwood.

YOOPER MATHEMATICS

To fully appreciate this story, you need to see things from the upper peninsula or Yooper point of view. Consider the creation of the earth, as a Yooper sees it.

In da beginning dere was nuttin.
Den, on da first day, God created da Upper Peninsula.
On da second day, He created da partridge, da deer, da bear, da fish, and da ducks.
On da third day, He said, "Let dere be Yoopers, to roam da Upper Peninsula".
On da fourth day, He created da udder world, down below.
On da fifth day, He said, "Let dere be trolls, to live in da world down below".
On da sixth day, He created da bridge, so da trolls would have a way to get to heaven.
God saw it was good, and on da seventh day, He went huntin.

Back during the lumber era, three men from down below, "trolls", arrive in a remote settlement in the upper peninsula, by railroad. They proceed to the hotel where they had wired for reservations. The clerk charges them $30.00 for the room, so each guest pays his share, $10.00. When the hotel manager arrives, he sees the charge, and tells the clerk that there is a mistake. These guests are from a major company, and are entitled to a discount. They should have been charged $25.00 for the room. The manager gives the clerk five $1.00 bills, and tells him to go to the room, explain the error to the guests, apologize, and give them the $5.00 refund.

On the way up to the room, the clerk starts thinking things over. These guests don't know about the special rate, and they are trolls after all. He decides he can give them a nice discount and make a couple bucks for himself. So, when he arrives at the room, he explains that because there were three people sharing the room, they were entitled to a 10% discount. Each man had paid $10.00, so the clerk gives each of the men $1.00. Now they had gotten a 10% discount, being charged only $9.00 each. Everyone was happy.

As the clerk went back to the front desk, he did the math. He had given each guest $1.00 of the

$5.00 and kept $2.00 for himself. So, each of the three guests had ended up paying $9.00. 9 x 3 = 27, add the 2 he kept, 2 + 27 = 29, and that is how $30.00 turned into $29.00 in the upper peninsula. The old timers say that this was an epiphany for the clerk. He had discovered that he had a talent, he could make money disappear. He decided to try to make a success of his talent. He moved to a bigger city and ran for office. Some say he eventually became a member of the United States Congress where he was able to make vast sums vanish.

WEBSITES

Getaways – www.michiganbackroads.com

Newsletter – www.travelinmichigan.com

Trails – www.upnorthmichigan.com

Unique Shops – www.michigangiftshops.com

Unique Lodging – www.backroadslodging.com

NOTES